# FROM BUSINESS CARDS TO BUSINESS RELATIONSHIPS

# FROM BUSINESS CARDS TO BUSINESS RELATIONSHIPS

## PERSONAL BRANDING
## AND PROFITABLE NETWORKING
## MADE EASY

### Second Edition

# ALLISON GRAHAM

John Wiley & Sons Canada, Ltd.

*Library and Archives Canada Cataloguing in Publication*

Graham, Allison Dawn, 1975–
    From business cards to business relationships : personal
branding and profitable networking made easy / Allison Graham. — 2nd ed.

Previously published as: Business cards to business
    relationships. London, Ont. : Elevate Press, 2008.
Issued also in electronic formats.
ISBN 978-1-11-836418-5

    1. Business networks.    2. Strategic alliances (Business).
3. Partnership.    I. Title.    II. Title: Personal branding and profitable
networking made easy.

HD69.S8G72 2012                    650.1'3                    C2012-901479-6

**Production Credits**
Managing Editor: Alison Maclean
Executive Editor: Karen Milner
Editorial Assistant: Brian Will
Production Editor: Pauline Ricablanca
Cover Design: Adrian So
Composition: Thomson Digital
Printer: Trigraphik LBF

John Wiley & Sons Canada, Ltd.
6045 Freemont Blvd.
Mississauga, Ontario
L5R 4J3

Printed in Canada

1 2 3 4 5 TRI LBF 16 15 14 13 12

*To my brother Tim, who taught me to dream big, persevere, and bring the impossible to fruition.*

*To my mom, Barbara Ann, whose unending kindness and generosity of spirit influence me positively every day. This book would not have been possible without her help and encouragement. For as many late nights as I've spent mulling over the words in the pages that follow, my mom has spent the same.*

*And to my dad, Robert James Graham (1944–2005), my best friend and sounding board for the first 30 years of my life. His wisdom continues to guide me. I wish he were here to share the journey.*

# Contents

THE THIRD PILLAR OF PROFITABLE
NETWORKING: PROCEDURES

# Preface

BEFORE I LEARNED how to network effectively, my life was dramatically different.

Working as a receptionist by day and a bartender by night, the idea of achieving meaningful success in the professional realm seemed like a pipe dream. However, that dream was turned into a reality thanks to the people who became part of my network.

At the time, I had no idea how powerful networking could be, but now I realize how incredible it is that each of us is just one contact away from having our entire life change direction.

**Each of us is just one contact away from having our entire life change direction.**

In a very short time I went from being "unconnected" to meeting thousands of people. Thanks to those connections and my hard work, I was able to create a successful and varied career as a newspaper columnist, frequent radio guest, local television reporter, and fundraiser raising hundreds of thousands of dollars for charities. I became an active volunteer in the community and eventually won a political nomination to run for public office. Best of all, I was able to create a successful business, Elevate Seminars + Strategic Development Inc. (www.ElevateBiz.com), teaching other professionals through conference speeches and corporate training how to change their lives and create success by getting connected.

None of this would have been possible without the incredible people who influenced my life both professionally and personally.

After leaving university I held a variety of jobs. I sold cars and makeup and even had an unsuccessful stint at selling knives. At one point I worked in a car-rental shop and then was a receptionist in a laser eye surgery clinic. Through it all I supplemented my income as a waitress and bartender.

By the time I was 25 I was in a rut and disappointed. While some would say my life was "fine," I was a long way from achieving the life I envisioned. Looking back, perhaps I was too young to be worried about making an impact in the world, but I knew deep down I was unhappy. My life lacked purpose and direction and I wanted more. Changes needed to be made.

Raising me in a small community, my parents set an example of how to live a rewarding, community-minded life. My father owned a food service business, excelled as an executive director for a provincial association, held leadership roles in various local community organizations, and was a municipal politician for many terms. My mother, a teacher, was involved in church and charitable activities. I fully intended to achieve similar success and felt I had the ability to do so, but I had no idea where to start.

One day I took a leap of faith and applied for a job as the executive assistant to the vice-president of a building-supply company. Not exactly an obvious place to find fulfillment, but my potential new boss was philanthropically inclined and happened to be the incoming president of the local Chamber of Commerce. I scheduled the afternoon off work at the eye clinic, put on my best (well, okay, my only) navy suit, and went to the interview. An hour later I was offered the job.

In the ensuing months, my life shifted. I watched my boss give back to the community, take many phone calls, go to umpteen events, and reap the rewards of his strong network. I quickly realized that I wanted to be the one with the network doing great work in the community—not just an assistant. Then, with another leap of faith, I left the company to find my own way.

So there I was, filled with big aspirations for a purposeful life, but unemployed—and unconnected. On my father's advice, I hesitantly called his lawyer's wife, Erin, who lived in my city. Dad was no stranger to networking and knew that one solid connection could lead to a new job. Erin and I knew each other from my childhood, but that didn't make the call any easier. I was intimidated because she was well known in influential circles, I was nervous because I hadn't networked for my own personal gain before, and I was shy because I lacked confidence and thus questioned why Erin would bother to take my call. These didn't add up to a great combination for someone who was unemployed. Eventually I mustered up the courage to make the call and I'm thankful I did.

Erin graciously invited me to a political "meet and greet" that she and her husband were hosting at his law firm that weekend. I didn't know what to expect so my parents, who were also invited, agreed to come to the event to give me moral support. I'll never forget that reception.

I collected several business cards and promised to connect with each contact the following week. While I was busy hunting for employment opportunities, my parents were volunteering me for various projects. By the end of that reception, "I" had agreed to get involved in a political campaign and join some mysterious charity gala committee. To start my gala work, I had to return to the law office the next Tuesday to meet the senior law partner so we could drive to the meeting together. Talk about venturing into unknown territory. I spent the whole morning getting ready—ultimately choosing to wear the same navy suit I had worn less than a year earlier for my interview.

On the ride to the meeting, I was so nervous that it was all I could do to keep from sweating through my suit while remembering to breathe as I listened to the classical music on his car radio. The whole time I questioned in my mind why this accomplished lawyer would invite me to work on this committee. I assumed he was thinking the same thing as I, the apparent mute, rode beside him. I felt completely out of my comfort zone. When we arrived, the committee members were incredibly friendly and welcoming. As we started to discuss the fundraiser, I found myself saying, "Oh, I know him; I'd be happy to make that call."

That's when I realized I had already started to build my network at my previous job. Since I'd left on good terms and had projected a professional image as an assistant, when I did call, the contacts were more than happy to help me collect auction items for the charity gala.

The contacts I met that day and at the political reception are still some of my best friends, business associates, and political supporters. Those few hours changed my life's path and led me to where I am today.

It didn't take long for the power of networking to become crystal clear to me. I was experiencing how one person could lead to another person who leads to the next person who positively influences your life. Soon, thanks to my new connections, I landed a job in the not-for-profit sector, became involved with several organizations, and earned a spot on a political party's provincial executive. Within 18 months my Rolodex went from having a few cards to being overloaded with hundreds of new contacts. A few years later that number grew to several thousand contacts.

During a phone call to someone in my newly established network, I learned that the *London Free Press* was looking for a columnist. Within a few months the paper published my first column. Four years later, I succumbed to my passion for politics and resigned from the newspaper to run in the 2007 Ontario provincial election. My party didn't win, but my involvement in the process was an incredible experience.

Building a network with thousands of quality contacts in such a short time wasn't an easy task. I remember one year that was especially hectic. In addition to running a company, writing my four weekly columns, working in radio and television, and volunteering for several organizations, I attended nearly 250 events. Add the effort needed to manage the network of contacts while finding time for a personal life, and you can imagine that my schedule was fairly intense. Working at that intensity level is not required to build your own ultimate network. In fact, I don't recommend that pace for anyone (myself included). But those interactions, combined with my varied professional and personal experiences, have given me the foundation for my consulting business, speaking engagements, current business column, and this book.

# Introduction

As a professional you likely attend, or plan to attend, business functions in an effort to expand your network. Why? Are you truly connecting with people or are you just putting in time? We spend our adult lives interacting with people to earn our living, but shockingly, throughout years of schooling there is no course dedicated to teaching us the specific skills needed to help us connect with others and build our networks.

Humans naturally engage in networking on some level, but when the word is formalized as a business activity, for some, it conjures a vision of calculation and manipulation. Proper networking elicits the exact opposite response. It's not a cheesy sales technique, but a genuine attempt to connect with others and to let others connect with you.

Sales trainers tell you to build your network to generate business leads. Job-hunting manuals advise you to tap into your network to get your résumé to the top of the pile. Company leaders push their junior associates to get "out there" and build their networks.

It all sounds great in theory, but how do you do this? Where do you go to build your network and once you're there, what do you do so that you're not just collecting business cards? What is the secret to turning those casual business-card contacts into long-term, mutually beneficial relationships?

Before I launched my training-and-consulting company, people would ask me for advice on how to get connected and I was happy to oblige. For some, a little advice was all the help they needed and they were off to build their network and achieve success. Others weren't so agreeable—or successful.

After showing up once or twice at events, they'd tell me networking doesn't work. They would lose sight of their reasons for wanting a strong network and quit. This result puzzled me. Of course networking works—I was living proof. I knew that networking, when done properly and professionally, is an amazingly powerful tool that will enable a person to achieve whatever can be imagined.

### Networking, when done properly and professionally, will help you achieve whatever you can imagine.

So why do so many professionals struggle to make networking work for them, while others find success with it? It became my professional mission to find tangible answers and help those struggling to fast-track their success by learning how to connect with the world's greatest resource—people.

As I studied people whom I perceived to be master networkers, it was clear most of them didn't consciously realize what they did to network so well. They found success by trial and error and by mirroring the behavior of their mentors. For them, networking just came naturally. Similarly, those who struggle with networking seem completely unaware of what they do to shoot themselves in the foot. Fortunately, some self-awareness and technique-tweaking are all it takes to get results that are better in line with your goals.

The information in this book will help you build your profitable and fulfilling network. The ideas presented are a culmination of extensive research into the best practices for networking and, most importantly, they are lessons learned from my personal experience interacting and connecting with thousands of people over the last several years.

If you are new to networking, you may find the information overwhelming, so read the book, do the exercises, and then revisit the concepts as you grow your network. Over time these strategies will make more sense.

If you have substantial networking experience, read the book with an open mind. Consider your own personal journey and how these concepts apply to you. Stick with what's working and fine-tune areas that need improvement to maximize your efforts.

As you read this book, you'll realize I am far from perfect. There are days when my foot finds a comfortable resting place in my mouth and I add another experience to my tally of embarrassing moments—some of which I share. Being prepared for the unexpected, accepting yourself for who you are at each moment, having a keen sense of humor, and forgiving yourself and others can go a long way toward helping you enjoy the process of building your professional network.

I wish you all the best as you work to create a profitable network. It will take time and effort, but it will be well worth the investment. I love to hear stories so please visit my website, www.ElevateBiz.com, to share your tales of success—and your blunders too. Also, you can visit the website dedicated to this book by scanning the QR code at the end of the book for worksheets and additional content.

# The First Pillar of Profitable Networking

*Perspective*

# 1

## The Power of Building a Profitable Network

How would your life be different if you were more connected? What would change? Would you make partner? Have more customers? Secure venture funding? Get a better job? If you're reading this book, there must be something that you're looking for over and above what you have today.

When I started my networking journey, I didn't know what I wanted to accomplish. I just knew I wanted a better life. I longed for purpose and was tired of barely making ends meet while living in the perpetual home-to-work rut. Instinctively I knew that if I wanted more, I had to get connected. At the time I didn't know what that required, but I was determined to learn the ropes. Really, I asked myself, how hard could it be to get connected? Apparently quite difficult if you don't know what you're doing.

Thankfully perseverance, hard work, and guidance from the right mentors meant I was able to go from basically unconnected to connected in a short time, creating a successful career in media, politics, business, and the charitable sector. None of it would have been possible without the influence of my newly formed network. There's no doubt that I had some talent and ability that helped me at each step in my career—just as I assume you do too. But having talent and ability doesn't matter if the right people don't know about them.

In order for people to choose you over your competition, you need to be on their radar. That's why networking is so powerful. When done correctly, it gets you on the radar of the right people. I'm living proof that anything you want to accomplish can be done by surrounding yourself with the right people and creating genuine connections with them.

While it won't happen overnight, with consistent and persistent effort it will happen. It's impossible to be a truly talented networker and be unsuccessful. At least, after interacting and connecting with thousands of people, I haven't seen that combination yet. Think about it: nothing happens without people making it happen. The more people a person is positively connected to, the more opportunities he or she will have. The law of averages means that getting connected will put you in an advantageous position both personally and professionally. Looking back, every exciting and challenging twist in my career was instigated by a connection with another professional. Most likely, when you look back on your life you will find the same to be true.

In their book *The Middle-Class Millionaire*, authors Russ Alan Prince and Lewis Schiff studied the behaviors and characteristics that separate the regular middle class from those who elevated themselves to achieve millionaire status. Their research identified four key elements that define the middle-class millionaire: hard work, financial savvy, persistence, and networking.[1]

In addition to being a fascinating read, this book underscored for me the importance of networking and its impact on the average person's ability to achieve optimal success. If your goal is to become a millionaire, then according to their in-depth research, mastering the art of networking is one of four proficiencies that can make that dream a reality.

Here's the catch: there are several different ways to network and some are more effective than others. The approach you choose has to match your personality, your circumstances, and your desired outcomes. Cookie-cutter attempts at networking can leave you frustrated. For example, a business networking group can be the source of endless referrals for one member and yet be an energy sucker for another. In the same way, a conversation starter can work for one person but bomb for another. These nuances must be recognized and embraced to create an optimal network.

The most powerful—and ultimately the most profitable—network is one that is genuinely aligned with your personality and is sustainable over the long term.

**The most profitable network is one that is genuinely aligned with your personality.**

---

[1]Russ Alan Prince and Lewis Schiff, *Middle-Class Millionaire: The Rise of the New Rich and How They Are Changing America* (New York: Doubleday, 2008).

Another catch is that there are several different ways to define a network. This book is not about collecting business cards and simply adding names to your database. You could have 10,000 names in your address book, but if you're not genuinely connected with those people and they don't know who you are, and vice versa, what's the point? There is a time and a place to have a massive list of names so you can send one-way communication from you or your company. That list shouldn't be confused with your active network that consists of mutually beneficial business relationships.

Online networking can also confuse the issue. It is an extremely important element of networking. Without a comprehensive online strategy, you are very likely missing networking opportunities. However, just as networking is one element of your overall business development strategy, online networking is only one element of your overall profitable networking strategy.

Regardless of your personality, your desired outcomes, or your current circumstances, profitable networking requires consideration in four different areas: Perspective, Personal Brand, Procedures, and Strategic Plan. As such, this book is divided into the Four Pillars of Profitable Networking. Each section builds on the previous one, so by the end of the book you will have all the tools necessary to develop your ultimate network. Just keep repeating the process and doing more of the right activities until you start reaping the rewards.

## FIRST PILLAR: PERSPECTIVE

In this section, you will learn how to shape your perspective on business networking by defining what it is and what it is not. It will help you solidify your overall goals and objectives, outline realistic expectations, and identify common mistakes that can keep you from truly connecting with others and getting results.

## SECOND PILLAR: PERSONAL BRAND

This is where we'll address and develop the Business of YOU to ensure you are attracting new business relationships by conveying the genuine, welcoming, professional image that is essential to your success.

## THIRD PILLAR: PROCEDURES

Procedures are the everyday networking elements that we're just expected to know, but are rarely taught. Mastering the fundamentals will give you confidence and add an extra notch of professionalism to your image. When used correctly and effectively, these basics can be your most valuable assets as you build your profitable network.

## FOURTH PILLAR: STRATEGIC PLAN

Once you're clear on your desired outcomes and have a solid perspective, are ready to share the Business of YOU, and have mastered the procedures, a strategic plan will help you decide the best places to go and how to create systems to turn your casual contacts into long-term, mutually beneficial business relationships. We'll also determine how online networking fits. Your strategic considerations are what will make your profitable network a reality!

Networking is the foundation for your success. Alone, it won't be enough to get you the results you want in business or for your career, but networking makes success easier and more probable.

You'll still need to make sales calls, but networking keeps you from making cold calls. You'll still need to run a solid marketing campaign, but networking makes it easier to get noticed. You'll still have challenges, but networking makes it easier to find solutions. You'll still have to submit your résumé, but networking gets yours to the top of the pile. You'll still have to deliver top-notch work, but networking gets more people to take notice.

Building a strong network is not rocket science. It's simply connecting with the right people and letting people connect with you. Once you've figured out how to connect with the world's greatest resource—people—you'll start to see the world's population as one big exercise of connect the dots. The possibilities for your future are infinite!

# 2

## What Does Having a Strong Network Mean to You?

IMAGINE THE POSSIBILITIES if you were to add hundreds of quality contacts to your personal network. Would achieving success be easier and faster? Yes, of course it would.

Networking is the foundation for whatever you want to achieve. It would be impossible for me to guess your specific motivation, but I suspect it falls into one of three categories: enhancing your professional results, improving your quality of life, or both.

The Fourth Pillar explores the importance of honing in on a few priority outcomes so you can strategically determine what activities fit best and will get you the best result. The good news is that although you may have a specific goal in mind, the benefits of networking have a domino effect. You can't experience one advantage without experiencing the others.

**Benefits of networking have a domino effect. You can't have one advantage without experiencing the others.**

Here are just some tangible and intangible benefits you can look forward to when you expand your network:

- having a sense of purpose
- living a happier life

- knowing whom to call when you have a need
- being in a position to help people by connecting them with others
- being seen as a leader in your community or industry or both
- making it easier to break into a new city or group of people
- experiencing company growth
- creating new friendships
- elevating your confidence
- eliminating the hit-and-miss application and interview process
- getting your charity to the top of the donor-request pile
- earning goodwill with your contacts
- amplifying public awareness
- seeing increased referrals
- knowing everyone in a room and having everyone know you
- generating new clients
- growing personally
- developing a positive reputation
- gaining professional development
- advertising through word of mouth
- creating company buzz
- finding mentors
- becoming a mentor for others

While throughout this book we're focused on building a profitable network, as you can see from the list of possible outcomes, the benefits of networking go well beyond pure profit. Depending on your circumstances, you may want to interchange "profitable" network with "strong" network. Either way, it means different things to different people. The most important question is this: What does a strong network mean to you?

## Networking rewards go well beyond pure profit.

Exercise: Close your eyes and imagine your life once you've built an exceptionally strong network. What are you hoping to achieve? Who do you want to know? What do you wish to accomplish that you can't without this strong network? Take a mental snapshot of your life with an amazing network. Write down your vision and keep your answer front and center in your life. Tape your answer to your bathroom mirror or beside your computer screen.

Identifying your vision and what you ultimately want to achieve will give you a point of reference that will motivate you as you build your network.

Years ago a friend said to me, "When my head hits the pillow at night, I want to be sure it deserves the rest." I thought this line captured the meaning of a purposeful life, so when I decided to take my life in a more fulfilling direction I wrote, "Deserve to hit the pillow" on a sticky note. Now I have a sticky note in my office that reads, "Make your mark," because it sums up what I want to do—make my mark on the world and help others do the same.

Your vision statement doesn't have to be profound—just something that reminds you of your long-term purpose. It should give you an extra boost of energy when you're frustrated going to yet another networking event.

This statement may change as you grow in your career and your priorities and perspective shift. Changing focus from the micro or day-to-day ("Deserve to hit the pillow") perspective to the macro ("Make your mark") perspective gave me the flexibility to move my life forward. Looking back, I wouldn't change either vision statement at those stages in my career, as they were necessary at the time.

The effort and focus required to create a solid network is different from what is needed to nurture a network after it's been built.

# 3

## Expectations

My consulting clients come to me because they have struggled, often for years, to create a solid network that leads to personal and professional fulfillment. They are fully aware they need to network and know it works for others, but haven't made it work for themselves—yet.

My job is to help them find the reason they're missing the mark and help them tweak their behaviors accordingly. Behaviors that hinder networking success are fairly universal and are usually one or a few of the following culprits. Each one aligns with one of the Four Pillars of Profitable Networking:

- not having realistic expectations and the wrong attitude (First Pillar: Perspective)
- not portraying a genuine, welcoming professional image that invites new relationships and encourages people to like you, trust you, and believe you are competent (Second Pillar: Personal Brand)
- not making it easy for people to know who you are, what you do, and what you have to offer (Third Pillar: Procedures)
- not having enough meaningful interactions with enough of the right people (Fourth Pillar: Strategic Plan)

To change results, we must first adjust our expectations. People who show up once or twice at networking events and get frustrated because they haven't seen tangible results from their networking efforts are setting themselves up for failure. Networking is not a quick fix. Getting to know people and letting them get to know you requires time. That's not to say that amazing things can't happen very quickly once you begin to interact with new contacts. They absolutely can. You never know whom you may meet and how your interactions with those people may change your life. However, it's best to have realistic expectations and practice patience as you build your profitable network and expand your circle of influence. In time, you will achieve your vision.

## Networking is not a quick fix.

Accept that you won't know everyone in a room the first time you walk into a function. Rest assured, however, that over time, with consistent and persistent effort, you will get to know more and more people and eventually feel like you belong. Expect that a room full of strangers will remain a room full of strangers until you meet and connect with them.

With networking, it is wise to adopt a slow and steady pace that will earn you a positive reputation and allow the natural development of solid relationships. After six months of business networking done properly and professionally, you'll create some momentum, make some initial contacts, and develop a sense of comfort and belonging.

## After six months you'll create networking momentum.

After 12 to 18 months of consistent and persistent effort, you will notice a significant difference in your professional network. That's when the magic really starts to happen. Within five years you'll notice your life has taken an entire shift for the better and you should be well on your way to embracing a profitable network, leaving your unconnected life behind.

About a year and a half ago I met with a contact for coffee. He was the sole advisor for a finance company's satellite office. He was quite frustrated with his slow start, so we discussed the importance of patience and revisited his vision for the long haul. He reluctantly accepted the reality that building his business network would take longer than he wanted.

Approximately six months ago I saw him at an event and he pulled me aside to tell me that after a year of consistent and persistent effort, business was falling into place. Just recently I saw him again and he said his business was booming. Finally, he felt his efforts were rewarded. Had he given up when he first had doubts, he wouldn't be reaping the benefits now.

A year or two may seem like a long time to wait, but do you plan to still be in business in 12 to 18 months? Your current investment will lay the foundation for future business relationships. The work required to build a sustainable network is nothing compared to struggling through your professional life "unconnected."

It takes six to eight casual encounters with someone before you hit his or her radar screen and he or she starts to "get" who you are. It takes even longer for you to generate a sense of trust and competency that will lead to significant relationships. Connecting on a deeper level than just saying "Hi" at a business reception can reduce this number, but even then it still takes multiple interactions with a new contact before you can expect to truly connect.

Think about how many people you've met, had lunch with, or even sat next to in a boardroom and yet have forgotten. Yes, this is a trick question because I'm asking you to remember people you've forgotten, but it makes the point.

Not everyone we meet in passing makes a lasting impression on us and vice versa. Expecting contacts to remember you after one or two introductions can be frustrating and can chip away at your self-confidence. It's not necessarily a reflection of how memorable you are, but rather the reality of society's hectic pace.

You may find that it takes longer to develop relationships with more-established leaders and accomplished networkers. They tend to have a healthy level of skepticism about newbie-networkers who flash onto the scene in a "here today, gone tomorrow" fashion. Over the years we've seen many who, after a whirlwind presence, drop off the face of the earth until they randomly resurface a year or two later. This kind of inconsistency detracts from a person's trust factor and diminishes his or her ability to connect with those who have a more consistent track record.

For better or worse, a person's true colors start to show after five or six months, so instinctively people tend to be guarded. It's easy for someone to put on an act for six months, which is why the six-month mark in any relationship is so critical. After that time, familiarity sets in, barriers break down, and true personalities start to show.

If you're like I am, and patience is not your greatest virtue, you'll be pleased to know there is a way to speed up the networking process. Do more of it! You can't force the natural pace of any one relationship, so to build your network faster you will have to increase the number of people with whom you connect. Some relationships will grow faster than others. I reaped the benefits of networking in an exceptionally short time because I jumped in with both feet, met a ridiculous number of people, and worked intensely to make it happen. As you read, you will get the tools to do the same, but remember that to gain credibility you need to be in this for the long haul.

## You can't force the pace of any one relationship.

Achieving your ultimate network could take years. How long depends on what you're willing to do to achieve it. Your ability to master all four pillars of profitable networking and put consistent and persistent effort behind your actions will make it happen faster. No matter how long it requires, take it from someone who has benefited extensively from the power of networking: it will be well worth your investment of time, energy, and money. Stick with it. Your efforts now will pay dividends in the future.

# 4

## What Networking Is Not

THE BEST WAY TO truly understand business networking is to first understand what it is not. While networking has caused people to waste excessive amounts of time and money, profitable networking, the kind taught in this book, will give you a significant return on investment. Networking is not just about showing up at events and schmoozing.

### Networking is not just about showing up at events and schmoozing.

Unprofessional networkers who confuse "networking" with "selling" create many of the misconceptions and negative connotations associated with networking. Far too often over-eager professionals blur the line between building relationships and entering the sales process without the right prequalifications. This provides an uncomfortable and frustrating experience for the person on the receiving end. When done properly and professionally, networking will open the door to new sales and referrals, but not if you force those desired outcomes on people you just met. Jumping the gun too quickly will raise the red warning flags for them; something just won't feel right and they'll be standoffish rather than open to developing a connection.

Going to networking events expecting to land new clients or sell your product sets you up for failure and frustration. This misguided philosophy permeates networking events. If, shortly after an introduction, a person rushes into a sales pitch without qualification of interest, need, or fit for the product or service being sold, then the opportunity to build a relationship is missed, because no one likes to be "sold" or feel "cornered."

## Going to events expecting to land new clients sets you up for failure and frustration.

Understanding that appropriate networking was different from jumping into the sales cycle was the turning point for a client who is the vice-president of an investment firm. Before we talked through his hesitations and he came to this realization, it was like pulling teeth to get him to engage in networking, even though his role required his presence in the community.

He was under the impression that each time he went out to an event, he had to catch a new client hook, line, and sinker. No wonder he wasn't comfortable with networking—that's a lot of pressure. Changing his perspective allowed him to genuinely enjoy the process of connecting with others.

This doesn't mean you should never enter the sales process after meeting a new contact. If a person expresses interest in your product or there is an obvious fit to collaborate on a venture, then yes, the sales process or an appropriate course of action should begin. (See Chapter 54: Categorizing Contacts.)

When this clear link does not exist, focus on taking the next step toward a long-term relationship rather than making the sale. Over time, as you learn more about each other and establish a deeper bond, opportunities to work together will likely present themselves naturally. In the Fourth Pillar we'll talk about where to go to be in target market–rich environments so when you *do* meet and connect with someone, there is a higher probability that he or she can become your client.

An associate dropped out of the "mainstream circuit" for a couple of years while he changed jobs and solidified his path. We ran into each other at a reception and I was sincerely pleased to hear he'd found passion and purpose through his new venture. He asked me to go for a coffee so we could reconnect.

The visit started off well. Then, the tone changed. I quickly understood our chat over coffee was actually a "sales" meeting—two totally different things. For 45 minutes he went into an elaborate sales pitch. He not only wanted me to become his client; he also wanted me to refer him to others.

Finally, when he came up for air, I explained that I wasn't a qualified prospect. This was crucial information he would have known had he spent time asking me questions, listening to my answers, or been up front about his true intentions when we booked the get-together. Worst of all, since my red warning flags were raised because I felt like I was being cornered and used, he missed the opportunity to have me as an ally in his new venture. By jumping to "forceful selling" rather than figuring out if I was a qualified prospect, he lost the long-term potential.

### Be up front and clear about your intentions for meeting rather than using backdoor, smoke-and-mirror tactics.

What is the likelihood that I'd go out for coffee again with him, let alone refer him to someone else? Zero.

Time is valuable, so to spend time listening to a pitch that had no relevance to me was simply annoying. I felt duped. If this had been my first exposure to the "networking process," I would have been completely turned off because he hid behind the guise of networking when truthfully he was in full sales mode.

On another occasion, a gentleman asked me to meet with him to discuss his business and to see if I could help. The expectation in this situation was clear from the onset so there were no uncomfortable sales pitches. Even though there wasn't a fit for me with his company, I was able and pleased to connect him with others who were better matched to his needs.

Two different meetings with different tactics, therefore different results. Be up front and clear about your intentions for meeting rather than using backdoor, smoke-and-mirror tactics.

Agenda-pushing also contributes to networking's bad name. In life everyone has his or her own agenda. The sooner you understand that your agenda is not the same as anyone else's, the easier it will be for you to take a step back and genuinely connect with people.

Another person's priorities are rarely exactly in line with yours. Hitting a year-end sales target or raising money for a charity would rank differently for the seller or fundraiser than for the potential buyer or donor. Accepting this natural variance in priorities will help you identify the appropriate pace for building a relationship. Pushing your agenda onto someone else is a surefire way to trigger their fight-or-flight response.

When inevitable year-end crunch times occur you tap into your *existing* network. That's not when you try to push new contacts into your master plan. There is a distinction between trying to close a deal with a new contact at a networking function and calling an established associate to ask to be referred to someone who may need your product or service.

Another negative networking image comes from those who try too hard. The overt social climbers who are anxious to arrive at a new station in life are easily spotted. People can smell a phony a mile away. People will resent you and your success when they sense that you're only out for yourself and that you will step on toes to get to the top. This may not be your intention, but if that's how you're perceived, then you have additional challenges to overcome.

If, before reading this book, you have developed a negative impression of networking, either because you have been on the receiving end of unprofessional networking tactics or because you have been guilty of blurring these lines yourself, the time has come to accept and erase any such connotations.

A negative impression doesn't diminish the importance of networking and the positive impact proper networking can have on your life. You can't change the past. The key is to focus on the future. Even if you feel like you've blown it, don't worry—you can recover.

Understanding common behavioral culprits that hinder networking success will help you avoid making these mistakes in the future and will set you on a path to become a master networker.

# 5

# Understanding Business Networking

ACCORDING TO THE ENCARTA DICTIONARY, by definition networking is the gathering of acquaintances or contacts; the building up or maintaining of informal relationships, especially with people whose friendship could bring advantages such as job or business opportunities.[1]

Bottom line: networking is all about connecting with others and letting others connect with you. From there, anything can happen. Profitable networking happens when you connect with people who are most likely to become clients or who can influence people in your target market.

### Networking is about connecting with others and letting others connect with you.

As we determined in the previous chapter, networking is not selling, nor is it a chance to push your own agenda. With that in mind, you may wonder how networking can generate business growth. To sell your product or service, you first need customers who are willing to buy what you are offering. Once they know your product exists, they must decide to buy from you instead of from your competition. There are various ways to engage people in this decision-making process, all of which when combined create a solid business development plan.

---

[1]Encarta Dictionary: English (North America).

Networking is one element of your overall plan. It's the foundation that will make all other elements more successful. When you have a strong network you can draw from it to complement your other business-development efforts.

One way to generate new business leads is through advertising. Not everyone has huge budgets to run massive ad campaigns to entice potential customers. It's the most costly option and if the other guy launches a bigger and better advertising campaign, you're out of luck. Online pay-per-click and social media campaigns have significantly lowered the financial barrier to entry, making it more achievable for the little guy to participate in advertising initiatives.

The beauty of networking is that it will complement an advertising campaign because the bonds you create in real life will naturally increase the likelihood that your message will rise above the noise. We can't underestimate the power personal connections have on a person who sees or hears a traditional advertisement. When they see the ad, their mind will connect the dots back to you.

There are certain industries that lend themselves well to macro-campaigns. Large companies, such as banks, can run huge advertising campaigns, but when it comes to earning the business at the grassroots level, relationships are more important. If you like and trust the bank manager at one branch, you're more likely to do business there, rather than across the street with the competition whom you've never met.

Another option to generate new client leads is cold calling. Not everyone is comfortable using these tactics, nor does everyone have the patience and staying power to work the numbers that these techniques require. You can expect less than 1 percent return from your investment when using these strategies in a traditional manner without incorporating the principles of networking.

Networking combats the cold-calling freeze because you can start your conversation by saying, "Our mutual contact, so-and-so, suggested I give you a call." This increases your potential for the conversation to begin and lowers the trust barrier compared to when it's a stranger calling.

In the end, networking is the most effective way to generate new business leads. Networking, done properly and professionally, will lead to new and existing contacts wanting to do business with you. It creates word-of-mouth buzz, attracts referrals, and generates loyalty. Networking opens the door so you can earn the business. As a person responsible for generating new business, what more could you want?

## Done right, networking creates word-of-mouth buzz, attracts referrals, and generates loyalty.

There are two overall objectives for business networking:

1. When you have a need, you know who to call, and when you call, he or she will want to pick up the phone to talk with you.
2. When your contacts or someone they know need your product or service, they will think to call or recommend you first.

Imagine how much easier life would be if, whenever you were looking for a solution, you only had to look to your personal address book to find the answer. With a strong professional network, you're only a couple of calls away from whomever you need to meet. Your relationship may not seal the deal, but it should at least get you in the door.

Better yet, imagine if your contacts immediately thought of you whenever a personal or professional situation arose for which you could provide the solution. It doesn't matter what you do, the principle remains the same. If you're an insurance advisor, financial broker, accountant, lawyer, car salesman, hairdresser, dance teacher, graphic designer, or any other professional with competition, you want to be sure that your contacts will think of you first as the potential solution provider for their needs and the needs of their contacts.

That's the power of profitable networking!

# 6

---

# Friendship versus Business Relationships

To UNDERSTAND THE ESSENCE of business networking, consider the famous quote by author and businessman Mark McCormack: "All things being equal, people will do business with a friend. All things being unequal, people will still do business with a friend."

With the changed marketplace, I actually don't think this quote has as much merit today as it did in the 1980s when McCormack first said it. (I hear the shrieking of business traditionalists everywhere.) As we've seen in the last few years, and will likely see in 2012 and beyond, accountability is crucial. Gone are the days of signing a contract solely out of loyalty. In the good old days, people would pay more or avoid looking at competitors' quotes just because they liked you. Today you'd lose your job or go broke if you ran a business that way.

Nowadays substance is a requirement. Being someone's buddy isn't enough to get and keep a contract. If you do get in the door based on a friendship or a favor, expect to deliver to a higher standard.

Most networking books teach that people need to know you, like you, and trust you to do business. I take it a step further. Prospects need to like you, trust you, and believe you're competent. My phrasing drops the "know you" because that's implied.

To make McCormack's quote relevant today, I would adjust it to say, "All things being equal, people will open the door for a friend. All things being unequal, you'll put your buddy in the awkward spot to open the door for you, but you shouldn't expect him or her to give you the business based on friend-ship alone, so be prepared to go out of your way to earn the business. Then, be prepared to deliver a higher quality product or service than the competition." Granted, saying it like that is not quite as catchy as the original quote.

Another way to make this famous quote relevant today is to adjust how we perceive "friend." It's doubtful that McCormack was saying you need to be best friends with everyone you hope will buy your product or service. That's not realistic, but there has to be something that distinguishes you from your competition. That something is a relationship. The balance is in determining the best depth of relationship that leads to business. It starts with a mini-bond, which you'll learn more about later in the book. It means you're not best friends, but you have connected enough to establish a sense of credibility. This connection includes a positive opinion along with a mutual understanding of each other's value, and consistent yet intermittent interaction. When needs align, that's when the door for a more in-depth business association can be pursued.

## There has to be something that distinguishes you from your competition.

I realize this may seem counterintuitive. You may be asking, "Isn't the goal to build deep, meaningful relationships with your buyers so you can get so close that they can't say no to you?" Well, yes, eventually. The ultimate goal is to solidify and create loyalty with your customers, after you've earned their business. Since studying and living profitable networking, I've come to realize there is a "sweet spot" of balance that maintains the professional boundaries while still feeling personal enough that you don't feel like strangers. Crossing the line and getting too close can be a deterrent.

Once people put you in the "friend" box, before they see you in a profes-sional light, it's difficult to go backward to learn your value as a professional. If you're already in the "friend" box and need to shift to the "professional" box, it can take more work to earn the business and get on your friend's radar screen as a legitimate contender.

It's amazing how many times I talk to professionals who complain that their friends, the people they see as their inner circle, go to their competition. There are three reasons this could be happening. First, they only see you as a friend. This means you will have to build your credibility as a professional and help them take notice of your ability to serve them, not only as a friend, but as a client too.

Second, they don't clearly understand what you do professionally and how well you do it. It is your responsibility to clearly communicate what you do and what you have to offer so they can make a decision one way or the other, which is the same with any contact, as will be shown throughout the book.

Third, they may be nervous about mixing business with pleasure. If this is the reason, you are in the official friendship box and need to decide if it's worth changing boxes. Drawing clear boundaries to manage these fears and expectations is helpful to set minds at ease.

One of my best friends changed roles inside a huge financial company that was on my original list of target firms when I launched ElevateBiz.com. As you can imagine I was pretty excited to hear she was now in charge of hiring speakers for the firm's conferences. "Woo hoo! I'm in," I thought. Ah, not so fast.

She did significantly more due diligence to hire me than she did hiring any other speaker, even though there was a strong fit with my message and their advisors and I was proven in the industry. She even had her colleague attend another firm's event to hear me speak so he could make the final decision. It was very stressful for her to hire me because of the optics of hiring a best friend. She feared if I didn't "wow" the audience, her judgment would be called into question by her superiors.

I'll never forget the day the session finally arrived. Five minutes into my presentation I looked at my friend, who was sitting at the "power table" at the back of the room. I watched as her boss leaned over to whisper in her ear. A look of relief came over my friend's face and so did a huge smile. When she gave me the two-thumbs-up signal, I could finally relax and stop worrying about her stress.

Even though, as a professional speaker, there is always pressure to deliver 100 percent every time you're on stage, having a best friend sign off on my invoice felt different. There was extra pressure because I was worried about her job as well as doing mine.

It can be difficult to shift the perspective of our closest family and friends from personal to professional. Therefore, I've found it's more advantageous to build solid genuine business acquaintanceships rather than deep, close personal friendships with our business contacts in the beginning. Once the business is established there is a chance those business contacts will turn into personal friendships too. That's great as long as the contacts see your credibility as a businessperson first.

The higher your professional "rank" or success, the faster this transition can happen. Let's say a vice-president moves into a new city and joins the local private golf course. Since he holds a high-level position, there is an inherent expectation of competence, otherwise he or she wouldn't be in that role. Therefore, when the new VP meets people at the golf club, there isn't as much of a hurdle, rightly or wrongly, to earn credibility as a professional. If he or she meets some new golfing buddies, they'll become fast friends and work is left off the green. A simple phone call to the office during the weekday and he or she can open the door. By the time a person has gotten to this level in their career, this process of meeting people, earning credibility, and transitioning to business when necessary is second nature.

It's our family and best friends who tend to imagine us when we were little, or focus on how we acted at the dinner party on Saturday night, instead of seeing us as successful professionals or entrepreneurs today. This boxed thinking can hold you back in business. So we need to find the balance in the depth of relationship that works best for you and your circumstances.

These can vary depending on industry, product, service, and the type of relationship and level of trust required. For example, if you're a financial advisor, you would naturally want to take care of your close family and friends to be sure they are well served by a trusted advisor. However, if you're not confident in your abilities, or if your family and close friends don't see you as someone who is competent in this area, then this business relationship won't likely happen—at least not until you've proven yourself in the real world. These people may give you a chance to show they support "little Jimmy" and his new venture by giving you a small piece of their portfolio.

It's easier to be seen as the go-to advisor in a business networking group where everyone's first introduction of you is in this role. If they accept you at face value as an advisor and grow to trust you as a professional, you're more likely to create a book of business from these contacts. Over time, as you prove your ability to manage others' finances, those in your inner circle are more likely to choose you to manage their finances too.

There are people who tell me their family and close friends won't buy from them and don't take them seriously. Most recently this happened with a woman who started selling costume jewelry. She's having a tough time moving her stock because the people she expects to support her don't see her as a businesswoman who will follow through. My advice to her is that there are lots of people who are her acquaintances who would be happy to become her customers so she should sell to them and forget the naysayers. When she does well outside her close-knit group, those closest to her will take notice and change their opinion.

**Naysayers in your life?**
**Go create success anyway.**

For those who network well, creating an environment where there is enough of a connection where prospects like you, trust you, and believe you're competent is a natural part of doing business. With some perspective, preparation, and practice, you too will achieve this sense of ease with your business networking efforts and find the best balance between friendship, acquaintanceship, and business that works for you.

The depth of personal relationship you have with someone can indicate the level of ease with which you can transition them into a business relationship. The following guidelines are generalizations, so depending on your situation and your chosen profession, it could magnify or minimize the resistance.

These are not intended to be excuses to ignore prospecting to your inner circle of family and friends. If at first they don't agree to become your client, and yet you believe you could work well with them, then you need to keep building your book of business and periodically check in with them to see if they've started seeing you in a new light and are ready to make the change.

These guidelines will shed some light on why certain prospects aren't jumping with enthusiasm to become your first clients as you embark on a new profession.

- Transitioning your inner-most circle of family and friends to professional when you start a new role: most difficult
- Friend to client: difficult, but depends on how big a gap there is between your friend's vision of you and your profession
- Professional contact to close friend to client: challenging and most time-consuming
- Professional contact to quality professional acquaintance to client/ referral source then to close friend: most profitable. This really is the magic formula for profitable networking.

Recognize that every personality and circumstance is different. You may be one of the lucky ones whose closest family and friends automatically see you in a professional light and open the floodgates to referrals and the transferring of their portfolios over to you (in the case of an advisor). Perhaps you sell a product that is commodity driven, so it's easy to sell because they may as well buy from you, since they have to get it somewhere. If so, that's fantastic. For those who aren't having as much luck professionally with their family and friends, that's okay. Go create success anyway!

# 7

## Education and Connection

IF YOUR CONTACTS CALL your competition instead of you, chances are you're missing the education and connection components of profitable networking. It's not their fault. The onus is on you to give them the information and the comfort level they need to choose to work with you.

It's unrealistic to expect that people will randomly pick up the phone to hire you if they haven't met you personally or heard of you through one of their trusted contacts. There are some commodity-focused businesses that can rely on customers secured through the Yellow Pages directory, but service professionals don't usually have that luxury. Regardless of the source for a client, you can't expect them to call if they don't understand what product or service you offer and recognize your value.

Networking is an exercise in education and connection. It is your responsibility to educate your contacts about who you are, what you do, and what you have to offer. It is also your responsibility to connect with others so they want to do business with you.

### Networking is an exercise in education and connection.

There are people who will circulate the networking scene for years, but don't clearly communicate who they are or what they do. They keep their "cards" close to their chest, possibly in an effort to avoid appearing pushy or too eager for a sale.

This subdued approach leaves money on the table because even though people may like you, they won't know and understand enough about what you do and what you have to offer to decide to do business with you.

Later in the book we will discuss specifics on how to communicate the Business of YOU and your services, but for now, just understand: it is your responsibility to make it easy for people to know who you are, what you do, and what you have to offer.

As you build your network, it's equally important for you to grasp who is in your professional network. Who do you know, what do they do, and what do they have to offer? Knowing who is accessible to you will make it easier for you to find solutions and connect others.

Once people know you, it's essential that they like you, trust you, and believe you are competent. Otherwise why would they want to do business with you?

If you walk around like a pompous diva, it's unlikely folks will like you. If you tend to exaggerate and over-promise at meetings then fail to deliver, it'll be tough for them to think you are trustworthy. If you're the drunken guy who flipped the golf cart at the last charity tournament, envisioning you as a competent investment advisor becomes a bit of a stretch.

## Project a genuine, welcoming, and professional image so people will like you, trust you, and believe you're competent.

To build a profitable network, you'll need to project a genuine, welcoming, professional image that will encourage people to like you, trust you, and believe you are competent. It can be difficult to look in the mirror and honestly dissect the image we portray. Habits formed over a lifetime can unknowingly block our ability to connect with others. Identifying and changing these behaviors, discussed in the Second Pillar, can be difficult, but doing so is imperative if you wish to connect with others to establish your ultimate network.

# Summary

---

## *The First Pillar of Profitable Networking: Perspective*

- Anything you want to achieve can be accomplished by surrounding yourself with the right people and learning how to connect with the world's greatest resource—people!
- You can become a master networker with proper perspective, preparation, and practice.
- You will experience networking momentum after 6 months of consistent and persistent effort. In 12 to 18 months you will be well on your way to reaping the rewards from your ultimate network.
- You need to meet someone casually six to eight times before you "get" who he or she is and vice versa.
- You can't force the natural pace of any one relationship. To build your network faster you have to increase the number of people with whom you connect.
- Be up front and clear about your intentions when meeting with contacts.
- Networking is not selling. It is an exercise in education and connection.
- Understand the classic mistakes that hinder business networking success so you can avoid them and maximize your results.
- There are two overall objectives for business networking: First, when you have a need, you know who to call, and when you call, he or she will want to pick up the phone to talk with you. Second, when your contacts need your product or service, they will think to call or recommend you first.

- Business networking is all about connecting with others and letting others connect with you.
- Networking is the foundation of your success. It is one part of your business-development plan, but done properly, it's the most powerful element that will complement all other activities.
- It is your responsibility to make it easy for people to know who you are, what you do, and what you have to offer.
- It is imperative that you project a genuine, welcoming, professional image that will encourage people to like you, trust you, and believe you are competent.

# The Second Pillar of Profitable Networking

*Personal Brand*

# 8

## The Business of YOU

PEOPLE FORM OPINIONS OF you the moment they meet you. Regardless if your paths will cross for only a moment or if it's the beginning of a wildly successful business relationship, the first several seconds of interaction lay the groundwork for what's to come.

Although it may seem superficial, the reality is, it's the initial reaction that sticks. It may only take seconds to make a first impression, but it takes a lifetime to break one. It's important to invest in your outward image to maximize your opportunity to make a positive first impression.

### People form opinions of you the moment they meet you.

There are several factors that contribute to the impression you make. Many of these are outlined in the following pages. Each factor, on its own, may not be the deal breaker, but combined, they will contribute to what others see, feel, and hear around you and, ultimately, the gut reaction other people have about you.

In addition to being aware of what kind of first impression you make, building your reputation over the long term is essential to forming deeper business relationships and keeping them. As you build your network and expand your circles of influence, the image you project will either help or hinder your networking results. By addressing your personal brand, or what I like to call the Business of YOU, up front, you will increase your ability to connect successfully with others. Taking steps to optimize the Business of YOU will enhance your networking efforts as well as make a positive impact on other aspects of your life.

No doubt you've heard the term *branding*. You can't take a marketing class without touching on the concept. Companies spend thousands and in some cases millions of dollars to develop corporate brands.

Marty Neumeier, author of *Zag* and *The Brand Gap*, sums up the concept of branding best: "A brand is a person's gut feeling about a product, service or company. It's not what you say it is—it's what they say it is. The best you can do is influence it."[1]

The irony is that companies spend all that money developing a corporate brand, but ultimately it's the people who represent the company who make the most significant contribution to influencing a company's brand. If a person answers the company phone rudely, the negative experience will naturally influence a customer's gut feeling about the company, regardless of what the latest advertisement says. Individual reputations have a ripple effect on a company's brand. Therefore, a corporate brand is really the sum of all the personal brands that represent it.

National and international companies are at the mercy of their local representatives. It's the people on the ground level who ultimately connect with current and potential clients—a scary thought for presidents of major companies with thousands of employees. Thankfully, for most of us, our livelihood is not in the hands of thousands, but rather in our own two hands. It's important to comprehend the enormous impact a personal brand has on your ability to connect and succeed.

Chances are you don't plan to budget millions of dollars to craft and communicate your personal brand like the major corporations will. We can, however, take the lessons from the giants and apply them to ourselves as individuals.

There are three main kinds of elements that contribute to a brand. Visually, the logo, color palette, and fonts contribute to what you *see*. Emotionally, the vibe of your promotional materials, customer experience, promise, and ability to follow through contribute to what you *feel*. Content such as tag lines, social media campaigns, and commercial lines by your spokesperson and mascot (spoken or written) contribute to what you *hear*.

While you can't control a person's gut reaction toward you or your brand, you can influence it by being aware of, and adjusting when necessary, what

---

[1]Marty Neumeier, *Zag: The Number One Strategy of High-Performance Brands* (Berkeley, CA: Peachpit Press, 2005).

others see, feel, and hear when they interact with your personal or company brand.

The smaller the organization, the more a person's reputation contributes to the public perception or gut feeling about the company. If you're the president of your own business, your company's brand is directly impacted by others' gut reactions about you. What individuals in your target market see, feel, and hear about you is what will form your reputation.

Don't underestimate the power the Business of YOU has on making or breaking your future. Each and every time you interact with others, they are forming an opinion about you—consciously or subconsciously—that will add to, subtract from, or reinforce whether they like you, trust you, and believe you are competent. These opinions are formed based on intangible perceptions that generate another's gut feeling about you, which equates to your personal brand, your company's brand, and, ultimately, your bottom line.

## Don't underestimate the power the Business of YOU has on making or breaking your future.

The key to developing your personal brand and optimizing the Business of YOU starts with self-awareness. What you have done in the past, what you are doing now, and what you will do in the future all impact how you are perceived by others.

Years ago, when I sold cars, my boss would say, "A customer's perception is his reality." How true. When you think about the impression you make, it's really not about what you think the impression is. The impression you make is what others think it is.

As we move through the coming chapters to develop the Business of YOU, your job is twofold:

- Identify your strengths so you can maximize what's working.
- Identify areas that need improvement so you can make adjustments and put yourself in a position to win.

The objective is not to change your personality. You are who you are and that's exactly who you need to be to build your network. The goal is to tweak behaviors that keep you from connecting well with others and growing a profitable network.

It can be a challenge to realize that there are parts of our personality not coming through as intended, especially when you mean well.

Major red flags with your attitude or behavior, such as bullying others or treating service staff poorly, need to be identified and corrected first and foremost. For the most part, making hasty changes in your life can be overwhelming and ineffective for the long term. It could cause you to focus too much on who you want to become rather than who you are.

Gradual changes work best. Incorporate one or two ideas every couple of weeks until you have achieved your desired image. Adjustments to optimize the Business of YOU are a balancing act, but over time, they will all fall into place.

# 9

# Overcoming Age Objections

AN INVESTMENT ADVISOR IN HER mid-30s asked me how, as a young professional, she can connect with older, more-established potential clients with money. She joked that you need gray hair to be taken seriously in the financial world. That's not necessarily the case.

Many young professionals I speak with share this sentiment, regardless of their line of work. Using age to avoid building a profitable network means you'll miss amazing opportunities. There is a wealth of wisdom to gain from the seasoned professionals who are anxious to impart their knowledge to up-and-comers. It may take a little extra finesse to relate to people outside your peer group, but it's definitely doable.

Having youth on your side can be a huge asset as you build your professional network. Starting early means you have years to develop and solidify relationships, plus, those who have been around longer appreciate a fresh face.

A professional network with a solid foundation will include people from all ages. It's a natural tendency to associate with people who are similar in age and station in life. These people will likely represent the bulk of your network, but don't be afraid to include interactions with people outside your natural sphere of influence. Expanding your horizons to connect with people from different age groups and walks of life is key to creating a profitable network.

Those who are more senior will offer great insight and perspective concerning life and success. Thanks to a few more years, they will have more contacts and a stronger network, plus a lot more experience to share.

At the very least, find one person who is older and wiser to act as a mentor as you grow your career. Connections with this person can ignite your networking success and your overall personal and professional growth. Some of my most treasured relationships are with people who are much older. Without their wisdom, counsel, and support, my past, present, and future journeys wouldn't be possible.

At 25, I was the youngest person in the room for my first charity-gala committee meeting. I felt completely out of my element. My saving grace was that at the next meeting I returned with a completed to-do list, which earned me credibility, and once you have that, age is no longer a factor.

When I was 32 years old I decided to run for a seat in the provincial legislature, but first I had to win the nomination from the previous member of the provincial Parliament, who expected to run for the seat again. It was a true clash between older versus younger, established versus new.

I always knew I would run for public office, but truth be told, I figured it would be later in my life. Circumstances determined it wasn't and, ultimately, it worked out in my favor. When I announced my intentions to run, a politically astute man said, "The only challenge I see with your candidacy is your age and the only thing that will cure that is time." As individuals, we have no control over our age. We only have control over what we do with the years we've lived.

## We have no control over our age, only what we do with the years we've lived.

Thanks to my substantial network I was surrounded by amazing supporters who were as committed to winning the nomination as I was, but still, we were up against a worthy opponent with decades of loyalty in the riding and two terms of actual legislative experience. In the end it was my nomination speech that tipped the ballots and led to my victory. Those who didn't know me saw that I was a credible candidate when I nailed my speech. As I calmly and confidently addressed the hundreds of people in the room, they stopped worrying about my age and focused on my message.

We didn't win the election, but it wasn't for lack of effort or enthusiasm. The months of campaigning were spent connecting with voters and earning a reputation as a genuine, hardworking candidate. When my age was mentioned, as it often was, my response was simply, "I'm not nearly as young as I look." That usually got a chuckle and then we would discuss pressing issues relevant to the political landscape of the day.

Hundreds of people of all ages helped with my campaign in varying capacities. One of the campaign's most dependable volunteers was 15 years old. His father was active politically and saw the value of his son getting experience in the political realm. Some were surprised to see such a young volunteer in the group, but as far as I was concerned, he was someone I could count on to always arrive on time, as promised, and with a smile on his face. When he interacted with people he was polite, articulate, and truly knowledgeable of the party's platform. His admirable qualities are rare in people at any age.

You see, it's not the age of the person that matters—it's whether you like him, trust him, and believe he is competent. Those are the necessary factors that influence and overcome concerns caused by obvious superficialities such as age. As a younger professional you'll have to work harder to prove you are credible. As an older professional, you'll have to work harder to prove you are still relevant and not stuck in the old world.

## It's not the age of the person that matters; it's whether you like him, trust him, and believe he is competent.

Success does not magically begin once you cross a specific age threshold. It can happen at any age. Sure, longevity can give you experience, perspective, wisdom, credibility, and a whole host of other benefits, but there are many people much older than you who still haven't scratched the surface on building their professional networks.

How you interact with people of various ages will change, depending on the nature of the relationship and the environment in which you are meeting. A formal black-tie affair elicits a different response from a charity volleyball game with a bunch of buddies from school.

As a young professional, the image you project, regardless of your environment, is even more important for earning credibility than it is for someone who is older. Dressing respectfully, articulating your thoughts clearly, and acting professionally will go a long way to connect you with the establishment. Playing with your tongue ring, sporting an overgrown goatee, or wearing pants with a waistline that drops to your thighs will make it difficult for people to see you as an equal in professional circles. Although these styles may fit with your usual crowd, to connect with others in business you need to be as relatable as possible. To be taken seriously all the pieces must fit, so make a point to maximize the Business of YOU.

You can be 55 years old, but if you're a crook you won't generate a feeling of trustworthiness. Similarly, if you're 24 years old and you deliver on your promises and present a professional image, you will earn your place as a serious contender in business.

On the flip side, there are some more established people who use their age as an excuse to avoid expanding their network and to rest on their laurels. Maybe they haven't had the kind of success they would have liked over the years and have stopped trying. They could be stuck in a networking rut, only talking with the same people rather than looking to new opportunities. These are the very people who should be making an effort to get connected—right now! Given the number of people being downsized and needing to create next careers, the more senior you are, the more imperative it is that you don't neglect your network; rather, you must continue to grow it. Who knows when or why you'll need it. It's never too late to build a profitable network.

If you're already extremely successful and have a strong network, then now is the time to contribute to the next generation's success. Embracing younger contacts will infuse enthusiasm into your life. Mentoring an up-and-comer can be fulfilling, and in the long run can open an entire new network of contacts for you.

Your age, young or old, should not be a deterrent. Wherever you are on the age spectrum, you need to back your image with substance if you want to achieve optimal results.

# 10

## You Never Know Who's Watching

ONE MORNING I WAS DRIVING into a coffee shop drive-through. The tight laneway with multiple entrances made the morning rush hour particularly challenging. As I was about to take my place in line, a man cut in front of me. Luckily, I wasn't in a rush, the sun was shining, and a favorite song was playing on the radio. I just smiled and waved him through.

Not long after, I was introduced to a gentleman at a formal event. He asked me if I drove a particular make and color of car. He was correct, but I was surprised he knew this information. He explained that he was the guy who almost crashed into me at the drive-through. He apologized for not seeing me and then commented on my friendly nature and positive response to what could have prompted a nasty fit of road rage.

Can you imagine the difference if I had opted for a negative—yet more common—response that morning?

The point is you never know who's watching from the sidelines. Each interaction with a contact, regardless of the environment, will add to, reinforce, or subtract from his or her opinion of you.

### You never know who's watching from the sidelines.

You never know who is standing behind you in a coffee shop line or sitting beside you at a hockey game. It could very well be the person you meet in the boardroom on Monday morning. It's not that you have to constantly watch over your shoulder; just be aware of the image you portray when you're in public and how your actions contribute to your personal brand.

You can test yourself by asking, "If my most important client saw me acting like this, would that be okay?" If you're getting drunk and making a scene in public on Friday night and on Monday trying to get an investor for your company, it is only a matter of time before the two worlds collide and your credibility is questioned.

Variations of the same story happen over and over again and chip away at the reputations of professionals every day. It doesn't mean you can't have fun; just keep your actions in check. The more people you meet and the wider your professional network, the more likely you are to run into people in casual situations. Your image isn't just generated in boardrooms and at networking functions; it's a culmination of all interactions between you and your contacts.

That doesn't mean you need to dress in a pin-striped suit seven days a week or put on full makeup before you go to the corner store; however, you do want to look presentable, act appropriately for the situation, and be courteous to others, regardless of where you are.

It's absolutely acceptable if you run into a business associate at the grocery store when you have two kids running in the aisle, a crying baby in one arm, a diaper bag falling off the other, and a pile of groceries overflowing your cart—that's life, that's genuine. Treating the cashier like she's a second-class citizen is a whole different story. This type of behavior will damage your personal brand.

## Each interaction will add to, subtract from, or reinforce the opinion others have of you.

When I worked in a laser eye surgery clinic, I gave a lot of latitude to patients because undergoing eye surgery is stressful and people respond to stress differently. There was one patient, however, who was very difficult. There were some complications with his procedure, all of which could be fixed over time. It got to the point where none of the staff wanted to deal with him. He was generally rude and overly demanding. We would all but flip a coin to see who would take his call and I was usually the one who did.

The next thing you knew, my career blossomed. I'd long since left the eye clinic and landed a coveted role as a columnist for the city's daily newspaper. Now this patient and I ran in the same social circles. The tables had turned. No longer was I a "little receptionist." In his mind, I now had the power of the pen.

We never discussed how we really knew each other, but every time I saw him, flashbacks of his impolite, unreasonable behavior crossed my mind. As much as he kept a smile on his face for the people he thought were important, I knew his true colors.

Adopting the principle to treat everyone equally and with respect at all times will ensure that you are never caught in this uncomfortable position.

I'm reminded of a similar experience that happened when I was a waitress fresh out of university. This story had a completely different outcome. There were two gentlemen who came to lunch every Friday. They arrived at noon, sat in the far corner booth and ordered a pitcher of Rickard's Red with a pizza to share while they talked business. They were always pleasant, even on the days when the restaurant was packed and the service was slower than usual.

Years later, one of the two gentlemen was a key member of the steering committee for the first golf tournament I worked on in my executive assistant's role. We were happy to recall our Friday afternoon conversations and since he and his associate had always treated me with respect, even though I was "just" a waitress, my gut feeling had always been, and continues to be, positive about the two.

# 11

# Your Ideal Personal Brand

DEVELOPING YOUR IDEAL PERSONAL BRAND is a process. To start, decide what you want your personal brand to be. When others have a gut reaction about you, what do you want their gut to say? Close your eyes and imagine the Business of YOU five years from now. What adjectives do you want people to use to describe you? Consider your mentors and those you deem to be the most successful in your field. Ask yourself, "Who has it together? Why does this person win my admiration? What qualities or behaviors do I appreciate and want to emulate?"

Review the list of adjectives below for suggestions. Remember, these words may not necessarily be used to describe you today but represent the ideal image you strive to project in the future.

- adaptable
- approachable
- assured
- aware
- calm
- community-minded
- compelling
- competent
- competitive
- confident
- contributing
- dedicated

- determined
- easygoing
- engaged listener
- engaging
- enjoyable
- environmentally friendly
- even-tempered
- family-oriented
- flexible
- forgiving
- genuine
- happy

- hardworking
- honest
- independent
- industry leader
- intelligent
- interested
- interesting
- mature
- non-aggressive
- patient
- polite
- positive
- professional
- put together

- realistic
- relaxed
- respectable
- respectful of others
- respectful of property
- sets others at ease
- sophisticated
- stable
- team player
- trustworthy
- values-driven
- welcoming
- well-rounded

Which descriptive do you value most? Once you've reviewed the list, prioritize the top 10 adjectives you want to present to others through your behavior. Next, narrow your top 10 to the top 5 qualities you want contacts to use to describe you.

Set aside your personal ideas for a moment and consider which are the most important qualities needed for your profession. Which ones will set you apart from your competition? Which determining factors will encourage people to do business with you? Are these qualities different from the five you initially indicated? Are your expectations of yourself on a personal level different from those in your professional capacity?

Now that you know what you are striving to achieve, you can move to the next chapter where we'll look at your current reality.

# 12

## Reality Check

Now that you've determined your desired image, it's time to consider the reality of today. Forget about what you want to portray; think about what you are actually portraying. What would it be like to meet you?

My clients cringe at this question because they are often afraid to honestly consider their answer. Don't be nervous; this is not a beat-yourself-up session. This is an exercise in self-awareness that will ultimately lead to self-improvement. Now is the time to identify any potential behavioral culprits so that you can work to improve them.

Close your eyes and imagine you were just introduced to yourself. What impression would you make? If you met yourself, would you want to do business with you? Trust you? Believe you are competent? Do the answers to these questions depend on the environment you are in at the time? Does the impression you make change with your mood?

### What would it be like to meet you?

How do others respond to meeting you? Do they engage in conversation with you or seem to not even notice you're there? Are they drawn to you? Are you approachable? Do you put people at ease or make them feel on edge? Are you interested and interesting? Are you argumentative or judgmental? Do you look professional or do you look like you just rolled out of bed? Do people back away from you? If so, are you invading their personal space by talking too closely or do you have bad breath or body odor?

Now that you're becoming aware of the Business of YOU, it's likely you will notice different reactions in different situations.

Write an initial list of adjectives that you believe portray you. Be honest. Next time you're in public take notice of how others react to you. Consider the descriptions below and whether they apply to you rarely, often, or depending on the situation.

- agenda-driven
- aggressive
- argumentative
- bitter
- controlling
- dishonest
- disorganized
- disrespectful
- diva-like
- dramatic
- gossipy
- hesitant
- immature
- impolite
- impulsive
- inappropriate
- incompetent
- insecure
- insincere
- interrogator
- interrupter
- invasive
- irresponsible

- judgmental
- messy
- moody
- nonchalant
- pushy
- self-absorbed
- selfish
- shy
- smelly
- standoffish
- stressed
- tardy
- unapproachable
- unaware
- uncertain
- unhappy
- uninterested
- uninteresting
- unprofessional
- unsure
- untrustworthy
- wasteful

Those are not the most pleasant adjectives, but unfortunately, each of us knows someone who fits each dreadful descriptive. Let's be sure that person is not you. These negative attributes will block your ability to connect with others.

Consider yourself in the good times and the bad. Sometimes your mood will determine the image you project at that moment. Although you may not normally be disrespectful to and judgmental of others, if you've had a bad day and your patience has worn thin, you could find yourself rolling your eyes at an innocent bystander.

This happens to everyone at some point, but knowing your personal triggers that cause your not-so-nice behaviors is the first step needed to avoid unprofessional mishaps. Understanding the importance of how the image you portray affects your personal brand will hopefully motivate you to keep yourself in check.

Write down your five most negative qualities that describe the reality of the Business of YOU, then compare this list to your ideal image list completed in the previous chapter. Now for the clincher: how far apart are your lists of descriptions, as in those you wish others would use to describe you and those they do use to describe you?

What are the consequences of portraying the image you currently portray? If you're rude and demanding at the dentist office, what happens if people in the waiting room overhear your comments? How would you appear if you treat your executive assistant inappropriately when your best client is nearby waiting to speak with you?

One by one, you can adjust your sails so everything moves together harmoniously. The idea of this exercise is not to become perfect, but to identify the potential idiosyncrasies that could hinder your ability to positively influence what people see, feel, and hear when they encounter you.

Recognizing shortcomings is just the beginning. Now you'll need to take action to achieve your ideal personal image. Focus on one or two key adjectives to change at a time. Make a commitment to address one issue. Once you've overcome it, move on to the next one.

# 13

---

# Why It Matters

In today's market, you can't afford to let your competition be the one creating mini-bonds with your current and potential clients. Solid relationships will help you maintain and gain clients in good times and when times are tough.

It's all about putting yourself in a position to win. As much as you may think optimizing the first impression you project and your personal brand are superficial places to invest your time and financial resources, they can make or break you. It's the reality of human nature. You can either fight reality or you can make it work for you.

Understanding the difference between your ideal image and your actual image is the first step needed to ensure a profitable network. Even if you don't want to admit it, your competition, for the most part, delivers a quality product that is comparable to yours. You're probably thinking that's not true—you deliver a far superior product or service. That's good. That's what you should believe, but your average contact doesn't know that for sure.

To people looking for an accountant, every accountant is just another numbers person. An insurance broker is just another person who sells insurance. A banker is just another banker. You and I know differently, but remember that a person's perception is his or her reality.

People will use your competition for many reasons. Perhaps they feel a stronger connection with them than they do with you. This could be through no fault of your own. Your competitors may have met them first and the relationship between them has longevity on its side, or it could be that you haven't met them at all. If that's the case, how could you expect them to think to call you over your competition? Or maybe, just maybe, your competitor makes a better impression than you do.

## Don't let your competition be the one creating mini-bonds with your current and potential clients.

Assuming you and your competition are comparable in product or service delivery, then the decision to choose to work with you over someone else is based primarily on emotion. It's the intangible reaction that is influenced by what others see, feel, and hear around you and your competition that will determine who they choose.

Whatever you project is what you will attract. Miserable people are magnets for others who will reinforce their misery. Similarly, those who are confident, happy, and welcoming will generally be surrounded by people with similar qualities. With whom do you think your clients and potential clients would prefer to do business?

To earn a client's business, especially to take it away from your competition, you will need to create a better mini-bond and comfort level with the client than they have with your competition. Ultimately, it's the solid professional relationship that will dictate where a person chooses to do business. The foundation for the relationship starts with your personal brand. Basically, if you don't project a genuine, professional, welcoming image, they won't give you a chance to create the relationship with them so you can earn their business.

# 14

## Personal Hygiene and Grooming

THE FOUNDATION OF YOUR IMAGE begins with the basics of personal hygiene and grooming. This should go without saying, and does for most, but after witnessing some pretty shocking mishaps in this area, it's obviously a challenge for some professionals to hit the mark of acceptability. Those who are clean, smell pleasant, and project a healthy, well-groomed image are more appealing than those who look and smell like they just rolled out of bed.

When you respect your own appearance, you will naturally seem more professional, confident, and welcoming. What shows on the outside is a reflection of what you are on the inside. What do you want your outward image to say about you as new contacts make snap first judgments? The obvious day-to-day activities that lead to a well-polished image can get lost in the midst of juggling family, friends, and career. Taking time to work on your image on a daily, weekly, and monthly basis is time well invested. Not only will you look better, you'll feel better too.

### What does your outward image say about you as people make snap judgments?

As a young professional, take an extra few minutes a day to create positive habits. I often joke that they must not sell irons to people under the age of 25. An associate of mine who works in human resources can't believe the number of young interviewees who arrive wearing wrinkled clothes. Give yourself benchmarks for day-to-day living. If an article of clothing has hit the floor or stayed in the dryer too long, unless it hits an ironing board or meets a steamer first, it shouldn't enter the public domain.

Similarly, if you have to sniff a piece of clothing to determine its eligibility as a clean garment worthy of public presentation and you hesitate—that's a surefire sign that it isn't. Send it to the cleaners.

Wash your hands after using the facilities, for your own hygiene and the comfort of the next person whose hand you will shake. I hear about this all the time after male colleagues return from the bathroom. "That guy didn't wash his hands" is not a good branding statement.

Men and women should keep their nails manicured and clean. There is no shame in a man going for a manicure, and women, it's a great way to take a little breather in this hectic world. At the very least, men and women should use moisturizer. Rough hands are uncomfortable to shake. Nail biters, try to break your habit. Yes, it's a difficult one to break but it's an important one to conquer. Bitten nails and cuticles are noticeable.

Women, if you haven't changed your hairstyle in five years, assume you need a new look. A bad hair day can dampen the spirits of any woman and unkempt hair can detract from the most attractive and appropriate outfit. Hair is a significant part of a professional image. No matter what your hair's natural habits, texture, or color, with the right stylist and hair products you can generate a great hairstyle.

If you constantly struggle with your hair, find a new stylist. The best way to find a good stylist is to ask someone with a similar hair type and a great style where she gets her hair done and what products she uses. Be sure to tell the stylist who referred you so she has an opportunity to thank her walking billboard. Ask your hairdresser for tips on how to style your hair professionally at home, between cuts.

Keep fragrance to a minimum. There are so many people with allergies, you never know who could react unfavorably to your scent. A light scent is okay, except in fragrance-free zones. Anything that can be "appreciated" from more than a foot away is too much.

# 15

## Professional Wardrobe

IT'S EASY TO REBEL and claim you don't really care what people think; therefore, you'll wear whatever you want to wear—that's your taste and it really doesn't matter. Well, actually, yes, it does matter. Your clothes are the outside reflection of how you feel on the inside. In today's society, when people make snap judgments to decide if they are interested in getting to know you on a deeper level, unfortunately the clothes you wear will be one determining factor in this decision.

That doesn't mean you need to head to the latest designer's store and blow your budget—quite the contrary. Professional wardrobes can be created on tight budgets. Plan to buy the best you can afford. Wardrobe development should be a proactive activity, not a reactive one. Start with what you have. Go through all of your clothes hanging in your closet. Do this with a professional style-conscious friend or an image consultant who knows and understands the image you want to portray.

Decide if each article of clothing adds to a professional image or detracts from it. Items that do not coincide with your ideal image should be given away, sold, perhaps through a consignment shop, or kept for social time.

**Your clothes are the outside reflection
of how you feel on the inside.**

Next, decide if the clothes in your professional pile are flattering to you. Do they fit well, match today's style, and convey an appropriate message? Once you know what you have that looks great, makes you feel good, and presents a professional style, make a list of what's missing and shop accordingly. When you plan to buy clothes that are flattering, you can avoid knee-jerk shopping sprees that waste money on items that won't (or shouldn't) leave your closet to see the light of day.

Many senior managers have asked me to stress, especially to the younger generation, the importance of wearing appropriate clothing to work. They share stories of the wardrobe disasters that candidates wear for job interviews, which make it really easy for managers to cross certain job seekers off the list.

As a rule of thumb, for job interviews or for job fairs where you'll meet potential employers, find out what the expected daily wardrobe requirements are at the company and dress a minimum of one notch above that. If it's a public company—for example, a bank—you could visit the location in advance to get an idea of what's expected and then dress above that. If it's a private office that's not easily accessible, then look on the Internet or ask colleagues for their opinions. When it's impossible to find out the reality, use your best judgment. If you would wear an outfit to a wedding, it's probably too dressy, and if you'd wear it out with your friends for coffee or to the bar, it's too casual.

If you struggle with your wardrobe, invest in the services of a professional image consultant. The financial investment will save you a sizeable amount of money in the long run. Here are some quick guidelines for women and men to use when developing a professional wardrobe.

## WARDROBE TIPS FOR WOMEN

Fewer quality pieces accessorized differently can expand your wardrobe substantially while keeping it current.

The more covered you are, the more professional you are perceived to be. Ask yourself, "If my significant other was talking with a woman dressed like this, would I be comfortable?" If the answer is no, change. You have more to offer in the boardroom than your breasts, so keep them covered. Don't dress for distraction.

This applies for formal business events as well. Just because the invitation says black tie, this is not the time to bring out your swankiest, sexiest dress that will have all the men gawking. Skirts should be kept to an appropriate length—when in doubt, err on the side of caution. To judge if your skirt is too short, sit in a chair in front of a mirror and cross your legs. Can you see up your skirt? If so, how far? That should answer your question.

Nylons are more professional than bare legs. Many women complain that nylons are uncomfortable, but really, even if they are sheer, your legs are still considered covered. Again, it comes down to knowing what image you want to portray. During hot months, wearing nylons to the office may not be necessary, but you should wear them to important business meetings and networking events.

### To judge if your skirt is too short, sit in a chair in front of a mirror and cross your legs.

You may have noticed that nylons do not repair themselves, so when they have a hole or run, throw them out rather than putting them back in the drawer. This will save you a lot of time and frustration in the morning.

Solid colors are more professional than small prints and designs. Stronger fabrics send a stronger message. Well-tailored suits can still look feminine and sophisticated. The goal is not to look like a man, but to look like a credible and professional woman.

Dark makeup is for when it is dark outside. Even if you don't normally wear makeup, add a little lip gloss and some mascara to add extra polish to your look. It sends a message that you care about yourself and took time to get ready. If you're not sure how to apply makeup well, head to a department store cosmetics counter or salon for advice.

## WARDROBE TIPS FOR MEN

Some would say men have it easy when it comes to dressing, but that's not always the case. Hopefully you either have a sense of style, a good tailor, or a friend in your life to keep you matched and appropriately dressed.

Business casual is still business first. Appropriate apparel is a shirt that requires buttons to close, a "pressable" pair of slacks and polishable shoes—not a T-shirt, jeans, and sneakers. Depending on the environment and level of business casual, you may need a jacket or sweater over the shirt. Golf shirts are casual.

Offices with business-casual dress codes that inadvertently become everyday casual can send the wrong message to clients. It could say that you're lax on your deliverables. Some firms are reverting back to a full business dress code because there were too many interpretations of business casual. If you don't want that to happen to you in your workplace, choose too dressy over too casual.

## Business casual still means business.

Your socks should match or be darker than the hem of your pants. When you walk into a room with dark trousers, dark shoes, and white or tan socks, the bright socks are the first things to be noticed. Your socks shouldn't walk into a room, you should. Dark suits are less memorable than light ones. Therefore, you can get away with wearing the same navy suit every other day, but wearing a gray or light-colored suit regularly will make you known as the guy in the gray suit.

If an invitation requests business-formal or black-tie attire, a dark suit is the minimum required. You will stick out as too casual if you wear a tan or gray jacket into a formal function. A tuxedo should really be worn for black-tie affairs.

Invest in quality tailored suits and add dynamics and personality to your wardrobe with crisp and fashionable ties, shirts, and accessories. If you're wearing a patterned shirt, keep your tie plain, and vice versa, unless you're in the advanced class. Generally speaking, too many patterns are distracting, not dynamic. If you're color-blind or color-deficient, find out what colors complement your complexion and work together. Don't be afraid to ask a clerk if that nice blue shirt is actually purple.

# 16

---

# A Smile

NOTHING IS MORE UPLIFTING and welcoming than a sincere, confident smile. Some people smile naturally; for others, getting them to smile is like pulling teeth. If you are enjoying yourself, take a moment to notify your face so it can notify others. A genuine smile can set people at ease and invite others to talk with you.

Subconsciously, a smile communicates that you're confident, engaged, enjoying yourself, approachable, happy, and compelling—and that's just for starters. A genuine smile will draw people to you. The next time you walk into a business function, look around the room. Whom would you prefer to talk with: the person who looks happy or the one who looks like she'll suck the energy right out of you? The difference between the two is usually a smile.

## A genuine smile will draw people to you.

An insincere, phony smile is demoralizing and insulting. It's so obvious when someone flashes a big toothy smile and then turns her head to have it completely disappear. This nuance completely changes the emotional reaction to meeting that person. If you've ever had it happen to you then you know how it can make your heart sink.

People who are gruff-looking by nature should take special note of their smile tendencies. Contacts may be intimidated by your stature. A smile can help dispel any potential intimidation.

Not only can a smile affect how others perceive you, it's an easy way to adjust your mood. When you don't feel like being around people or are unhappy, smile and see how it changes your entire demeanor. Your subconscious won't know the difference.

If you are self-conscious about your smile, figure out why. Would you be happier if you had your teeth bleached? A year of braces is less painful than a lifetime of hiding a smile.

# 17

## Eye Contact

EYES ARE THE WINDOW to the soul. If you truly want to connect with others, give them this subconscious opportunity to see right into you. A person who constantly avoids eye contact insinuates shiftiness, lack of interest, or low confidence.

Proper eye contact communicates that you are listening. Have you ever tried to talk with someone who is watching television? The TV watcher may hear what you are saying, but it's tough to believe he or she is really listening to you or caring about what you have to say.

Connect with someone by making and maintaining eye contact; not in a phony, stiff, hypnotic trance way, but in a genuine "I'm focused only on you right now" kind of way. The most effective way to snub someone is to avoid eye contact when he or she is trying to talk with you. When you fail to genuinely acknowledge people with solid eye contact, they will get the loud and clear message that you're not interested in talking with them. If that's not the message you want to send, then make eye contact.

### Connect with someone by making and maintaining eye contact.

A friend of mine quizzes his kids about people's eye color after they interact with them. It's a great way to teach kids—and adults—about making eye contact. When was the last time you noticed a casual contact's eye color?

When outside, if possible, avoid wearing dark or mirrored sunglasses, as they make it difficult for people to see your eyes.

Wandering eyes are the ultimate subliminal insult. Insincere politicians are notorious for this and so are people who are really not focused on you. The eyes wander when a person is not engaged in the conversation because he or she is actually scanning the room for the next, more important person. Even if that's not the intention, that's what wandering eyes communicate.

If you see someone in your peripheral vision and accidentally allow your eyes to wander (sometimes it just happens), simply acknowledge it. "Oh, there's so-and-so. I was really hoping to catch up with him. Do you know him too or shall I introduce you?" Or you could just open your entire body position to allow for the passerby to enter the conversation. By acknowledging your wandering eyes, you will dispel any feeling of disinterest while making the person you were talking with in the first place feel like he is still in the loop.

This book highlights North American customs; in other parts of the world, eye contact between the sexes or with superiors would be inappropriate. If you are working in an ethnically diverse community or abroad, learn the customs so you can be aware of what is appropriate and what is not. You can adjust your behavior accordingly to accommodate your client or simply recognize why someone may react differently than you'd expect.

# 18

## Authenticity

By DEFINITION, YOU CAN'T fake being authentic. You don't need to look in a dictionary to figure that out—it's easy to spot a phony person. They are obvious and usually not very well liked. Unfortunately, these are the same people who are so consumed with putting on airs that they don't realize others can see through their act.

It's the person who pretends to like you and then rolls his eyes as you turn away. Or the person who has a frown, followed by a huge fake smile that immediately fades when heads are turned. Or the person who offers an insincere invitation for lunch.

Don't think for a moment the contact or others who are close by don't notice such unwelcoming, insincere behavior. Genuinely happy interactions with people will elicit a smile that will naturally stay on your face even after the conversation is finished.

Contacts will see through a phony façade eventually and, really, putting on airs must be exhausting. At the end of the day, only you will know the real you. Not being true to yourself will hinder your ability to connect genuinely with others and, most importantly, keep you from being truly happy.

**Depending on the environment, your behavior will change, but your personality and core character should not.**

Consistency in character is essential to projecting an authentic image. If you treat everyone equally and stay true to your personal values and beliefs, this shouldn't be a challenge. Depending on the environment, your behavior will change, but your personality and core character should not. The Business of YOU remains constant.

Keep compliments sincere, appropriate, and gender neutral. The general rule is that it's safe to compliment a woman's taste, but not her genetics.

A lack of confidence or a feeling of inadequacy will cause professionals to pretend to be something they are not. Trying to figure out who everyone else wants you to be is impossible. Each person's opinion will be different. When it comes to building your professional network, the best person you can be is you—authentically you.

# 19

## Approachability

Body language tells tales—long, accurate tales.

Standing with your arms crossed and a scowl on your face doesn't make you seem inviting. Ignoring people around you to only focus on the "important" people makes you seem snobby—and snobs are rarely liked, especially by other snobs.

Standing in a corner, moving quickly through a crowd, avoiding eye contact, turning your back to someone, looking others up and down, and acting judgmental are all conscious or subconscious ways to tell contacts to stay away.

To project an approachable image, keep an open stance with arms uncrossed and a smile on your face. For those who fidget and keep their arms crossed: to avoid this, try to keep one hand in your pocket, squeezing a Kleenex, or clasp your hands behind your back to keep open body language. It's not ideal, but it keeps you from being distracting. If you fidget with anything that makes noise, such as clicking a pen, please stop.

Look like you want to talk with others. Keep your eyes focused at eye level rather than looking to the ground, which is a surefire way to avoid engaging people. Slow down when you walk through a crowd to give people a chance to catch your attention.

**The more comfortable you make others feel, the more likeable you will be.**

Whenever possible, face the crowd rather than put your back to people. Obviously, in crowded areas, when you're in the middle of where everyone is mingling, you're bound to have your back to someone.

For the most part, meeting strangers is an intimidating experience, particularly for those who are shy, so projecting a welcoming personality will set others at ease. The more comfortable you can make others feel, the more likeable you will be.

Once you engage with someone, square your shoulders to that person so you are directly looking at each other. This sends the message that you are focused at that moment, which allows for a deeper conversation to happen, even in busy environments.

# 20

## The Tone and Pitch of Your Voice

CHANCES ARE THE TONE AND PITCH of your voice are the last things you think about unless you're a professional speaker or singer. Regardless, your voice still matters. How we sound affects how we are perceived.

For the average person, this is not a real challenge, but for some, an unpleasant voice can make it difficult to attract contacts who will like you, trust you, and believe you are competent.

When I get very excited telling a story, my speech becomes fast-paced and my voice becomes high-pitched, which makes it difficult for others to understand what I'm saying. Now that I'm aware of this, I take a deep breath and make an effort to ensure my speech remains at my normal pace and my voice is at a comfortable pitch so others can follow what I am saying. The content of my story may not change, but people's ability to understand it will.

**To determine if you have unfavorable voice habits, your best bet, aside from recording yourself, is to notice others' reactions when you speak.**

To determine if you have unfavorable voice habits, notice others' reactions when you speak.

Do you speak too softly? This may very well be the case if people are always leaning toward you and squinting while you speak to hear you better. If conversation partners seem to tune out when you speak or don't engage in the conversation, it may be that they simply can't hear you.

A soft speaking voice makes it difficult for people to hear you and can give others the impression that you are timid, insecure, or hesitant. Using an audible, firm, and confident voice will present a much more professional image.

At the opposite end of the spectrum, do you speak too loudly? Do people several feet away always seem to be eavesdropping or looking at you as if your conversation is infringing on theirs?

A hearing loss may be the reason you speak so loudly, in which case, consider getting your hearing tested. Once hearing loss is ruled out as the cause for your loud talking, simply follow the sound advice my big brother would tell me: "Take it down a notch."

Loud speakers can be especially annoying in restaurants and at meetings. Have you ever sat beside someone who thinks he is whispering, but everyone turns to look at the two of you? It's especially annoying when a speaker is talking from a podium.

Another way to tell if you're too loud is to notice your conversation partner's body language. Are people constantly telling you to shush or looking around to see who may be overhearing you? A boisterous laugh can give the impression that you are immature, seeking attention, obnoxious, or purposely allowing others to hear what you are saying.

Do you mumble or talk too quickly? The clarity of how you say something is as important as the volume at which you say it. Do others find it difficult to understand you? It is a good indication that this is the case if people routinely say "Pardon?" or, even worse, "What?" and ask you to repeat yourself. If so, make a serious effort to slow down and pronounce your words clearly.

When you are nervous, perhaps at the podium giving a speech or meeting someone you admire, the natural tendency is to rush your speech, so it's important to be mindful of your pace.

Most voice problems can be solved with some self-awareness and self-discipline. People with extreme voices can hire a voice coach to help them become more audibly pleasing.

# 21

---

# Sense of Humor

SHARING A LAUGH WITH SOMEONE is an excellent way to create a mini-bond. Laughing drops the defenses, has amazing physiological effects, and can make a new contact seem like an old chum. A moment of true laughter can stem from a situation, a funny comment, or a joke.

When it comes to jokes, it's a tough call. Some people can tell jokes; some people can't. It's important to acknowledge in which category you fit. If you're not sure, assume you can't.

There is a fine line between appropriate and inappropriate humor in business settings and, unfortunately, as people become more familiar with contacts, the lines become even blurrier. When you are at a business function you should be acting in a professional capacity on behalf of your company. Know your audience and err on the side of caution to ensure you are presenting a positive, professional image at all times.

**There is a fine line between appropriate and inappropriate humor in business settings.**

Once you've decided that a joke is appropriate for your environment and audience, determine if the length of the joke can survive the hustle and bustle of an event. Jokes that take longer than three sentences to complete are very difficult to deliver effectively in mingling environments because you're bound to be interrupted before you deliver the punch line. It's a common occurrence for people to restart the same joke to include newcomers or because people lost track of the plot. Unless the story is really engaging, you'll lose people. Generally their attention spans are short.

Save inappropriate jokes for close friends in nonbusiness settings. Running the risk of offending someone is not worth the laugh you may garner. Until you have a reasonable understanding of a contact's personality and particular sense of humor, anything that could be taken out of context is too risky. Stay clear of anything that is said at the expense of someone's race, religion, sexual orientation, or other generalization.

Making fun of another person is never acceptable. It may have you laughing at the moment, but in the long run your professionalism is shot. If you are heard making fun of someone as he or she walks away, it's only natural for the person who hears to wonder if you'll do the same thing when he or she leaves. Those ever-so-important like and trust factors become diminished.

Sexual innuendos, although common, are inappropriate in the business community.

# 22

## Confidence: Part One

### *Understanding It*

THERE WERE OCCASIONS, not too long ago, when I was so nervous talking in front of crowds that my voice would crack, my hands would shake, and my face would turn bright red.

The worst was watching the faces in the crowd respond to my unease at the podium. Half were probably thankful they weren't addressing the crowd and the other half, I'm sure, were wondering who gave me a microphone. I can still remember the pained expression on one man's face as I introduced a political speaker—to this day I cringe whenever I think about it.

Then there were other times when I sounded like a professional. Cool, calm, and collected as I charmed the crowd.

Thankfully I realized the difference was preparation. When I knew the key points I wanted to make and was clear about my purpose for speaking, I appeared confident because I was confident. Slowly but surely, this idea helped me overcome my fear of public speaking. Still—to this day—if I'm put on the spot to speak in public about a topic other than business development and profitable networking, I'm a nervous wreck.

**Developing confidence has been the single most important personal transformation that has had an impact on my career.**

In terms of public speaking, the best advice I received was to ask myself before every talk, "What do I want the audience to do, think, and feel because of hearing me speak?" This is such a huge confidence boost because it reminds me to focus on the needs of the crowd rather than inwardly analyze how I'm doing.

Thank goodness I learned that, otherwise running for political office and launching a professional speaking career would have been impossible.

Confidence isn't just necessary on stage; indeed, the same lack of confidence was true for me at events and with networking. One friend jokes that I had to create systems to network because otherwise I was too intimidated to do it—and she's bang on. At times I would walk into a room and feel like a fish out of water, while at other times I felt like a part of the crowd. This was because I lacked confidence when I didn't know people or have a reason to be in the room. Overcoming this was not an easy task.

For me it took several years of stretching my comfort zone to find true confidence, but it was well worth it. From my perspective, developing confidence has been the single most important personal transformation that has had an impact on my career. It's important to find the sensitive balance between confidence and a flashing ego. Confidence, or what I interpret as being comfortable in your own skin, will set others at ease. You will exude welcoming qualities and people will see you as someone who has it together.

A healthy dose of ego can have the same benefits, but displaying too much ego can annoy people, repel them, and make them feel inferior. Ironically, projecting an intense ego or an extraordinarily high opinion of yourself usually masks a secret lack of self-confidence—so don't be too intimidated by the pompous folks in the crowd.

People are naturally drawn to confident people. Those who radiate confidence have that certain charisma about them that is usually followed by success. A lack of confidence can be misinterpreted as noninterest or unapproachability when actually the problem is that you're just feeling out of your element.

True confidence allows you to take your eyes off yourself and focus on others. Confidence lets you take risks. It keeps you from second-guessing your every move. I remember years ago hearing a speaker say, "There is the speech you plan to give, the one you give to the crowd, and the one you give to your steering wheel on the way home."

That's what my entire life felt like. I would meet someone and then replay in my head all of the stupid things I said during our conversation. It would drive me crazy. I spent more time worrying than actually enjoying the moment. Perhaps you can relate.

## True confidence allows you to take your eyes off yourself and focus on others.

Finally I came to the conclusion that I had to deal with my confidence issues once and for all. I was not prepared to spend my life living in the shadow of some fictitious perfect image I constantly strived to be rather than accepting who I truly was.

Without confidence, it's difficult to connect with other professionals. Time spent worrying is time that could be used to build relationships. There's a difference between not having self-confidence and being nervous about stretching your comfort zone. It's normal to be uneasy about taking the next steps as you build your business network. Walking into a room filled with strangers can cause the most confident professionals to hesitate, myself included.

Just recently I was in another city at a function where I knew I'd only know a few of the expected guests. I was early; all of my friends were late. This left me gulping for air in unfamiliar territory. It had been a long time since I had that sinking feeling of "Oh my goodness, who will I talk with?" My first instinct was to wait in the car until the people I knew arrived. Then I remembered my own advice, got out of my car, stood up straight, put a smile on my face, and walked into a room full of people I did not know—yet.

My first conversation was with one of the organizers at the reception desk. I genuinely congratulated her on what seemed to be a successful event judging by the number of people in the room. (The people at the registration table are always safe bets if you're looking for conversation partners to break the ice. However, don't talk with them for too long because they will have others to welcome to the event.)

Next, I made my way to the bar. Then, with drink in hand, I noticed a group talking nearby. I made eye contact with one of the members of the group. This allowed me to walk over and say hello. By the time my associates arrived I'd already met several people and had been given three new business cards. I would have missed these opportunities if I had opted to wait in the car for my friends.

# 23

## Confidence: Part Two

### *Developing Networking Confidence*

THOSE OF YOU WHO ARE truly confident, feel free to skip to Chapter 25. However, in my experience, all of us can use a little boost in our self-confidence in order to enhance our networking skills, so you may wish to keep reading this chapter and the next.

Looking back on my personal journey, I know there were three key elements that drastically affected my confidence level. They are the same three words that I mentioned earlier as important to building your ultimate network: Perspective, Preparation, and Practice.

**Confidence takes time to build,
so be patient with yourself.**

To build confidence, you need to change your perspective on matters that influence your confidence. Once you grasp a few simple realities of human nature, it's easier to gain perspective and become more comfortable in the networking world.

The greatest realization for me was that most of my fears were unwarranted. Even when embarrassing moments happened or when I thought I made a less-than-stellar impression, I still managed to function and found that more often than not, most people didn't notice my faux pas at the time or, if they did, didn't remember it after the fact.

You'll find aspects of preparation throughout this entire book. Dealing with your personal brand and the Business of YOU, developing a solid professional image, mastering the fundamentals, and having a proactive strategy are all parts of preparation. By dealing with these first and foremost, you will be confident that you are making a great first impression, allowing you to focus on others.

Confidence takes practice. The more business networking you experience, the easier it will be, and the more confident you will become. Genuine confidence will give your networking efforts a sense of ease, and allow you to enjoy the process. By continually challenging yourself to stretch your comfort zone, you'll eventually broaden your boundaries. Confidence takes time to build, so be patient with yourself.

# 24

# Confidence: Part Three

## Seven Steps to Elevate Your Confidence

### STEP 1: IDENTIFY YOUR VALUE-ADDED QUALITIES

The first step to elevated confidence is to understand why you deserve to be confident. What valuable qualities do you bring to relationships? What do you offer that could benefit others and make them want to know you?

What makes you great? What benefits come with knowing you? What makes you special? Why do you think your friends are your friends? What are your strengths? Why would someone be lucky to know you? Don't be shy. This list is for your eyes only.

When you make your list, don't focus on superficial attributes. If the best you can write about yourself is that you have good hair, one bad-hair day could make your confidence fall flat.

Write down all of your positive qualities. Don't stop till you've listed a minimum of 20. Every morning read the list as soon as you awake. Internalize It. Believe It. Exude It.

### STEP 2: IDENTIFY YOUR FEARS AND CONFIDENCE ZAPPERS

Write down all your fears and confidence zappers. You can download a Confidence Chart at www.BC2BR.com that can help you work through these steps. What do you not like about yourself that makes you feel insecure? Are you afraid you'll say something stupid? Are you concerned you'll trip and fall flat on your face? Do you fear people will laugh at you? Do you worry that you don't have enough education or that you're not good enough? Are you unhappy with your image and feel others won't like you? Do you even know why you lack confidence? It's impossible to develop confidence until you understand why you don't have it in the first place.

In this step, do some real soul searching and decide exactly what it is that keeps you from feeling truly confident. What expectations do you have for yourself? Where do you feel you fall short? If you feel you don't belong, why? Write it *all* down. Be honest with yourself. Again, this is for your eyes only.

## STEP 3: IMAGINE THE WORST-CASE SCENARIO

What if your biggest fears became realities? What are the consequences if the worst-case scenarios were true?

Let your imagination roam as you take every fear and confidence zapper and play the scenarios out in your mind. Write your answers in the Confidence Chart you started in Step 2. What if you said something stupid? What would that stupid thing be? What if you fell flat on your face? What if people laughed at you? What if you don't have enough education? What if you're not good enough? How will your life be affected if the worst-case scenario actually played out?

Now ask yourself, how likely is the worst-case scenario to happen? Are your confidence zappers legitimate reasons for people to not like you or for you to feel unworthy and out of place? Consider people you know. Can you think of anyone who has experienced the very things that worry you? How were they affected? Are they still liked by others or were their reputations ruined?

Chances are it'll be difficult to find anyone who has actually suffered and not recovered from the very concerns that keep you from living a confident life. Accept that your fears are unlikely to come true and if they do, accept that they are usually not the issues that will influence others' opinions of you. This will allow you to stop worrying about the fictional worst-case scenarios and focus on connecting.

Review this list again in 24 hours. Time will give you some perspective on the worst-case scenarios and their likelihood of ever occurring or impacting your life. Once you've re-read your comments, you'll realize that things are rarely as bad as they seem at first glance.

## STEP 4: FIX IT OR ACCEPT IT

Now that we've identified what's holding you back, we need to get you out of your own way so you can build your ultimate network. To do this, you have two options to develop confidence: either fix your concerns or accept them.

What keeps us from having true confidence is our inability to fix or accept our shortcomings and ignore unjustifiable fears. This enables these perceived inadequacies and worries to hold us back from achieving optimal success.

In Steps 2 and 3, you listed all the barriers that keep you from feeling truly confident. To successfully overcome your personal hurdles, you need to find your own solutions. Look at each challenge individually.

Are you willing to accept the consequences of the worst-case scenario if it happened? If not, do you have the courage, attitude, and commitment needed to fix the very confidence zappers that keep you from connecting with others?

**What keeps us from having true confidence is our inability to fix or accept our shortcomings and ignore unjustifiable fears.**

There are some things about ourselves that we can't fix, leaving acceptance as the only choice. For each item that you've identified as a confidence zapper, decide if you can fix it and, if not, how you can accept it and move forward.

What advice would you give your best friend to deal with these potential challenges and fears? Now, as difficult as it may be, it's time to take your own advice.

For example, if one of your confidence zappers is that you don't feel that you dress professionally enough to be taken seriously, that's an easy one to fix. Find a friend who has a professional style. The two of you can go through your closet and pull together outfits that are professional and ones that are not. Mix and match different suits and accessories so you have several different outfits (even if they come from a few basic pieces). Having professional outfits organized in advance will give you confidence and make it easier to get ready in the morning. Problem solved.

Other confidence zappers aren't as easy to fix. This is where perspective is so important. Do you really think people will like you less because of your height or weight, a speech impediment, or your older model car? Likely not. Most people are too busy worrying about themselves to worry about what qualities and possessions you do or do not have.

If something is of specific concern to you, ask yourself, "How can I divert focus from this shortcoming so people see my strengths?"

There are normal risks to life, such as the potential to fall down in front of a crowd or to say something stupid, but you can't let those fears hold you back from having huge success. I always figure, minimize the risk and have faith that you can recover from those less-than-impressive moments. (See Chapter 25: Recovering from Embarrassing Situations.)

Decide for each confidence zapper if you will fix it or accept it, and record your action plans on the Confidence Chart.

## STEP 5: STOP APOLOGIZING

The best way to zap your confidence is to continually apologize for your short-comings. It keeps you from focusing on your strengths. Catch your negative self-talk. For every negative comment you make about yourself, contradict it with two positive thoughts. It's an excellent habit to develop that will eventually change your perspective about yourself. For those who have significant negative self-talk habits, the book *The Happiness Trap: Stop Struggling, Start Living* by Dr. Russ Harris is really helpful in teaching you how to diffuse the negative stories we keep replaying in our heads.

> **For every negative comment you make about yourself, contradict it with two positive thoughts.**

If you've ever said or felt that you don't want to waste someone's time by talking with him or her, you have a confidence problem. It is not average behavior to apologize for communicating with someone. I hear people say it all the time: "I don't want to bother you . . . but . . . can you . . .?"

Truly successful people are not "bothered" by people talking with them. They become "bothered" when someone does something that is bothersome, such as pointing out you are bothering them. Your existence is not bothersome. Saying please and thank you once are enough words when asking for input or a favor.

## STEP 6: TAKE YOUR EYES OFF YOURSELF

Be conscious of yourself, not self-conscious.

Deal with the Business of YOU. Accept or fix your confidence zappers so you can focus on other people and their needs. Take a genuine interest in others and adopt a "pay-it-forward" attitude. Always ask yourself, "What can I offer this person besides the product I sell? How can I make someone else's day better? What can I do to help others?" Good deeds have a way of boomeranging out of the blue.

When you take your eyes off yourself, you will be less likely to feel self-conscious. This will free you to embrace potential business relationship opportunities and friendships that are staring you in the face. The simple act of genuinely listening to a person can make the difference of whether or not a person feels valued when he or she is around you. When you make others feel valued, you will be happier as a result.

The most successful people are usually the most down to earth. We all put our pants on one leg at a time. It may be a cliché, but it's the truth. We all have feelings, fears, wants, and needs. Everyone wants to belong. That's part of life. When we put other people on pedestals, no wonder it's difficult to connect with them—they're too far out of reach. It's only natural to feel self-conscious or intimidated by them if you hold them to such high standards. At the end of the day, people are just people.

## Be conscious of yourself, not self-conscious.

If another person is at a business function, you already have something in common. You've both gone to the same place. Everyone in the room is there to meet new people and reconnect with current contacts. If they didn't want to interact with people, they would have stayed home.

Before you go into a function, review your list of 20 reasons why others would be fortunate to connect with you. This exercise will give you a last-minute confidence boost.

## STEP 7: MAKE IT HAPPEN

The best way to expand your comfort zone is to give yourself mini-challenges. Encourage yourself (okay, force yourself if need be) to do things at the top edge or outside your comfort zone. Sometimes you've just got to get out of your own way to let something happen. When you survive big or even small leaps of faith, you slowly, but surely, gain confidence.

Remember when you were a kid and you would get scared in the middle of the night? Then you would start playing that 1-2-3-go counting game over and over until you finally got the nerve to run to your parents' room.

**Until you truly feel confident, your best bet is to straighten your back, get dressed in your best outfit, and put a smile on your face.**

When you finally ran through the house to safety, you were relieved the boogeyman missed you, at least for that night. Gradually, you overcame your fear and understood that the boogeyman doesn't exist. Then, instead of wasting all that valuable time worrying about fictional worst-case scenarios, when you woke up from a nightmare, you'd just shake it off and go back to sleep.

Mastering events and interacting with other professionals can be tackled in the same way. Sometimes you just have to make it happen and trust that the confidence-zapping boogeyman is a nonissue.

Until you truly feel confident, your best bet is to straighten your back, get dressed in your best outfit, and put a smile on your face. To others you will appear confident and, surprisingly, acting confidently will help you feel more confident. Your subconscious won't know the difference.

# 25

## Recovering from Embarrassing Situations

Now that you've identified the biggest fears that zap your confidence, I need to tell you that sometimes embarrassing moments do happen and things can go wrong.

As you interact with more and more people, unavoidable embarrassing moments are bound to happen. This fact shouldn't shake your confidence or keep you from getting out there and making things happen. These are the very moments that can be turned into opportunities. Trust me, as a klutz and a speak-before-she-thinks type of person, I've had more than my share of embarrassing moments.

How you react and recover in these times of tribulation will affect how others perceive you.

### As you interact with more people, unavoidable embarrassing moments are bound to happen.

For example, if a waiter spills food all over your suit, you have two options. You can accept it, wipe yourself clean, and make some refreshingly comical remark to make the waiter feel comfortable. Or you can freak out, give the waiter a blast, call the manager over to the table, demand dry-cleaning money, and stomp out of the restaurant as if you are the only person who has ever had food spilled on a suit.

I've witnessed both extremes. The first option makes you a much more likeable person. Clothes will come clean—your reputation as someone who overreacts while making others squirm may not.

After I had volunteered for a political party, an associate suggested I run for the party's provincial executive. I was still getting my feet wet in these circles. I knew it could be a rewarding experience because I'd grown up around politics, so I stretched my comfort zone and accepted the challenge.

Not long after, the soon-to-be-president of the executive was hosting his campaign launch party in Toronto. It was a perfect opportunity for me to meet the party "bigwigs" in hopes of winning their support.

Before I started mingling, I went upstairs to use the restroom. Upon my return, I paused at the top of the stairs to get a feel for the room below. I made eye contact with a group of gentlemen at the bottom of the long staircase. Knowing full well these were the go-to guys I needed to impress and that all eyes were on me, I ever so confidently began my descent into the packed restaurant while maintaining eye contact with the group.

About halfway down the stairs, I discovered my strappy silver sandals were not the sturdiest footwear choice for a sweaty summer day and down I went—all the way to the bottom. I will never forget the look of horror on the gentlemen's faces as I bounced my way to ground level.

The momentum propelled me into the group. Perched on the leg that still had feeling, I offered a one-legged half-curtsy as I extended my arm to shake each hand. As if nothing happened, save of course the dripping blood from my ankle, I said, "Hi! Allison Graham. Nice to meet you."

Needless to say, my "graceful" entrance and recovery helped me win the election to the provincial executive. Later I was told that before that night, the men weren't sure they would support my nomination because they hadn't worked with me yet, but they figured anyone who could recover so graciously and quickly from such an entrance was destined to be in politics.

Yes, I could have made a U-turn, run upstairs, and called it quits after embarrassing myself so publicly. Thankfully I didn't, because in the end, the accident worked out in my favor. Good can come from bad situations when you look for the silver lining.

**Good can come from bad situations when you look for the silver lining.**

As you build your network, expect to be caught off guard. A sense of humor and the ability to laugh at yourself can be endearing qualities and help people relate to you. It's impossible to relate to "perfect" people. Plus, knowing that you can recover from whatever life throws at you will take away pressure to be perfect and add a sense of confidence to your demeanor.

If becoming a specialist at recovering from mishaps doesn't appeal to you, then feel confident in knowing that most people won't even notice when you embarrass yourself and, if they do, they won't care or remember.

Aside from the gentlemen who later ran my campaign for the executive, I doubt any of the 400 people in the room have any recollection of my disastrous fall seven years ago.

If you did something wrong or said something you wish you could erase, learn from the experience and avoid making the same mistake again next time.

When bad things happen, it's natural to replay your regrettable moments in your head. Reliving your not-so-fine blunders then beating yourself up doesn't help you build your confidence or your profitable network. Doing this can drive you batty and keep you from putting yourself out there. In these situations, I find it helpful to write about the embarrassing moments in my journal. Playing it out "officially" seems to bring perspective, as does time.

Think back on your professional career. What were your most embarrassing moments? How did you recover? Did those situations affect you profoundly? Was there anything positive that came out of the experiences? Were you ruined? Probably not.

## THE RULES OF RECOVERY

1. If an embarrassing situation arises and it's accidental, do your best to find humor in the situation and go with the flow.
2. If you've done something wrong, recognize it, admit it, apologize appropriately, and move on. Avoid gushing or over-apologizing because you run the risk of making the scenario worse and drawing negative attention to yourself.
3. If the situation is someone else's fault, accept the apology and cut the person some slack. Your easygoing nature and forgiving approach will add to your appeal both as a person and as a professional.
4. If you notice someone having an embarrassing moment, try to distract from the situation or find a way to save him or her. He or she will be eternally grateful. To connect with others, you want them to feel comfortable around you. When someone has done something wrong or feels embarrassed, that's an opportunity for you to be the bigger person by setting him or her at ease.

# 26

## Building Your Reputation

ONCE YOU'RE KNOWN, you'll be known for something. It's up to you to decide if that's a good or a bad reality. A positive reputation has the potential to open unlimited doors for you, while a negative one can close them quickly.

The first step to consciously building your reputation is to determine if you are, in fact, trustworthy or competent. Convincing others of something that is not true won't last long, if it happens at all. If you determine that you are neither trustworthy nor competent, then you're going to need more than this book to help you. For our purposes, let's assume that you are both a trustworthy businessperson and you are more than capable of delivering a quality product or service.

Every interaction with contacts will add to, subtract from, or reinforce the opinion others have of you. Over time situations will arise where contacts will hear about you and interact with you. Each occurrence contributes to a deeper consideration of your existence, which ultimately reflects on your reputation.

Mastering a positive first impression and being conscious of how you make others feel when they're around you will affect whether or not people like you. Your reputation, developed over time, will determine if people trust you. Your communication of topics related to your profession is how people will learn to believe you are competent.

Have you ever heard someone say, "I wouldn't trust him as far as I could throw him"? That's a perfect example of a person's reputation being communicated. What are the chances you will choose to do business with that person?

As you expand your business network, you can't expect everyone will like you and sing your praises at every available moment—that's not a realistic expectation. However, there is a distinction between disliking someone because personalities clash and believing and actively sharing your view that a person's core character is flawed.

> ## There's a distinction between disliking someone because personalities clash and believing and actively sharing your view that a person's core character is flawed.

Time is your best ally in developing your reputation. If your ultimate goal is to be seen as a mover and shaker in your industry, then you need to know this will not happen in an instant. Chances are, there are already movers and shakers in your industry. Not only do you need to create a name for yourself but also you'll need to earn your stripes.

Once you get noticed and expand your circles of influence, others inside and outside your industry will take a more objective look at who you are, what you do, and what you have to offer before you'll settle into your place within the industry's natural structure.

The key to a positive business reputation is to deliver on what you promise. If you exceed expectations you will be perceived as a real go-getter who is true to your word.

Repeatedly, people—especially young, naive professionals—get caught making unrealistic promises to make themselves sound important. Then, when push comes to shove, they can't deliver. When they drop the ball, inevitably someone has to pick it up and that major blunder can detract from the very essence of the professional image they're trying to achieve.

If you find yourself in over your head, the best approach is to come clean as soon as possible. No one minds if a committee member can't sell five tables to a charity ball. That's understandable. However, you lose friends and influence when you break such news to the gala organizer 24 hours before the event by returning 50 unsold tickets.

No one expects you to be Wonder Woman or Superman. They do expect you to do what you say you're going to do.

This rule applies to the small things as well. If you say casually, "I'll send you her contact details," make sure that when you return to your office, you actually send the contact details. Most of the time people just spew random comments like "I'll get that information to you" or "I'll tell so-and-so to call you," then never follow through on their promises.

How many promised lunches do you have rolling around in the universe that you know will never happen? Unless you truly want to have lunch with a person, don't bother making the suggestion and running the risk of losing your credibility.

"Let's do lunch" statements flood the airwaves of business networking functions daily and yet, these invitations rarely materialize into real meetings. Each time you make false promises, your insincerity chips away at your credibility and ruins your reputation.

> **Each time you make false promises, your insincerity chips away at your credibility and ruins your reputation.**

It's just as respectable to say "I'll call you to discuss it" or "Why don't I pop by your office for 15 minutes for a coffee?" rather than "committing" to a meal or a golf game or any other activity in which you don't intend to partake.

Consistency is another major contributor to building trust and a positive reputation. An inexperienced networker who flashes onto the scene for two weeks and then disappears for six months makes it difficult for others to find him or her credible. Sure, sometimes life happens and you get busy; however, building your network is either a priority for you or it isn't. You make the call. It does less damage to do nothing than to start and stop over and over again.

That doesn't mean you need to be out networking seven nights a week, 12 months a year. When your to-do list is overloaded and you simply can't focus on building your network, it's important to maintain it. Take one hour each week to touch base with key contacts via telephone, e-mail, or social media so they know you haven't dropped off the face of the earth.

Proving you're competent comes by doing—and doing well. Commit to delivering good service and over time your reputation will be that you do just that. Positive word-of-mouth buzz will be created and then everyone will want to work with you. Social media also provides a significant platform for you to prove your competency in your profession. Depending on your industry, a blog, writing for publications, or thoughtful status updates could give you a chance to show your stuff.

There is nothing that can damage a budding business relationship faster than failing to deliver when a person recommends you to a contact. Connecting people, especially for the first time, is a giant leap of faith. Inevitably the person who makes the referral feels responsible until the project is completed and completed well. If you fail to deliver as promised, you will lose your new client and your referral source.

In business, sometimes things go wrong. Everyone knows and accepts that. It's how you handle the mishaps that make all the difference as you develop your reputation. Open and honest communication is the best way to salvage potential blowups. Develop a recovery plan so you and your team know what to do when things do go wrong. It's a simple flow chart that shows the steps you'll take to salvage the relationship and make things right. Some restaurants do this well. Imagine your meal is cold when it comes to the table or there is a hair in your food. How could the restaurant make it right? Here's an example of a recovery plan.

1. The server accepts full responsibility, apologizes, and takes appropriate actions to correct the error.
2. The manager comes to your table to apologize.
3. He or she removes the appropriate menu item from the bill or adds a free dessert.
4. The manager offers a gift certificate for your next visit.
5. The owner follows up with a phone call or e-mail after the fact to be sure you are satisfied with the outcome.

Consider your product or service. What are the types of actions you can take when things go wrong? Accepting responsibility and apologizing should be the first step. After that, you have to figure out what makes most sense for you.

Once you have built a reputation and are seen as your industry's go-to person, you must stay the course to maintain your positive reputation: provide competent service, stay true to your word, and remain visible.

# Summary

---

## *The Second Pillar of Profitable Networking: Personal Brand*

- A good reputation is a powerful asset as you build your ultimate network. Do everything you can to earn and protect a positive reputation.
- A corporate brand is really the sum of all the personal brands that represent it. You can't control how people feel about you; you can only influence their perception of you by projecting a positive image.
- Today in business, age barriers are essentially nonexistent. Personality, perception, and performance count much more than age.
- No one expects you to be ON all the time, but when you're in public, ON is best and neutral is the minimum standard. It's too risky to be OFF in public—you never know who's watching you.
- Determine what image you want to portray so you can strive to achieve your ideal personal brand.
- You want to positively influence and shape what people see, feel, and hear when they interact with you and your company brand.
- How you say something is as important as what you say. Be aware of the tone and pitch of your voice.
- Sharing a laugh can strengthen a bond. Be sure jokes and comments are appropriate for your audience.
- Most confidence zappers are imaginary threats. We have the power to get a grip on ourselves and gain control so we are free to become the self-confident individuals we have a right to be.

- Be conscious of yourself, not self-conscious.
- We're human, so no one is perfect. As a result, mistakes, accidents, and blunders happen. Recognize when you've made a mistake and know the rules of recovery.

# The Third Pillar of Profitable Networking

———— ∽ ————

## *Procedures*

# 27

## The Fundamentals

MASTERING THE FUNDAMENTALS OF NETWORKING will give you a strong foundation on which to build your professional network. In some cases these may seem like obvious minor details, but in fact little things can make all the difference. The good news is that the fundamentals are easy to learn.

As we go through school and start our careers, the focus is on learning the specific skills required for our industry rather than learning the simple things that make life easy and give us a professional edge.

As you read this section you may discover that you've missed the mark on one or more of these skills. Even if you've been doing all of them wrong before reading this book, don't worry—you're in very good company. I've witnessed countless senior executives fumble with the fundamentals.

Learning these skills will help you focus on connecting with others rather than worrying about what fork to use or on which side of your body to put your name tag. With a little practice these skills will become automatic and give you a confidence boost because you won't have to second-guess your every move.

Once you've mastered these skills, don't expect people to "ooh" and "ahh" from across a crowded room. Actually, most people won't even notice when you're doing something right. The specifics will become nonissues.

If you mess up and do something wrong, that's when people in the know will notice.

When you master these procedures you will exude confidence and present a positive, professional image. Even if it's on a subconscious level, people will notice that you seem to have it together, which will contribute positively to your overall personal brand.

Keep in mind these ideas reflect North American traditions and when visiting other cultures you are encouraged to learn the best practices for those settings.

# 28

# Handshakes

It's REMARKABLE THAT in a professional networking book, I would have to tackle such a seemingly basic form of communication, but unfortunately, I've received enough bad handshakes to know it's a top priority. A handshake is the subconscious communication of your character.

What does your handshake say about you? Does it give the impression that you are disinterested, unsure, unprofessional, overbearing, controlling, wishy-washy, or insincere? Is your handshake solid, floppy, hurried, painful, or blasé?

The ideal handshake joins two hands for a firm, web-to-web grip for two or three pumps and is then released. Your wrist is kept strong.

Eye contact is imperative during this entire process: it completes the communication. Yet so often, eye contact is missing altogether or it lasts for a mere half-second before you or your shaking partner look somewhere else. When I meet someone who doesn't look me in the eye when shaking my hand, I want to grab his chin and shift his head back front and center to me and say, "Hello, yoo-hoo, we're in the middle of something here. If you're too important or uninterested to connect with me for five seconds, why did you shake my hand in the first place?"

## A handshake is the subconscious communication of your character.

There are probably many reasons at the root of this lack of eye contact. I suspect that for some it's a lack of confidence. Others aren't aware that they're not fully engaging in the handshake.

Create a mental trigger so that when you touch a person's hand for a handshake, you automatically look him or her in the eye.

Take special notice of eye contact (or the lack of it) in group situations. This is where professionals often fall short, even those who are good at making eye contact during single-handshake introductions. There is a false sense of urgency to meet and greet when others are waiting their turn for an introduction. Rather than focusing on each individual, the greeter feels compelled to take a sneak peek at the next hand he is about to shake. Greet each person in a group dynamic as you would in a one-on-one setting.

Eye contact will increase your ability to connect with the other person. Make a conscious effort to make eye contact on your next opportunity to shake someone's hand and notice the difference.

As a professional in North America, one must accept that it is customary to shake hands. If you have a cold or are extremely germophobic, simply deny the handshake, citing that you want to protect the other person from getting whatever illness you have. Take the onus on yourself rather than making the other person feel like he is the problem.

At a recent conference, a colleague told me the story of how, immediately after shaking a new contact's hand, the gentleman pulled out a sanitizer bottle and used it right in front of him while they were still talking. How insulting! That's completely unacceptable.

I've not kept an official tally, but I would suggest about 50 percent of handshakes miss the mark on total professionalism. So basically, there is a 50-50 chance that you are good at handshakes. Those aren't great odds. So let's tip the scale in your favor. To do that, we'll first take a look at some classic handshaking mistakes people make.

## THE FLOPPY-FISH HANDSHAKE

This handshake speaks for itself. There's just no life to it. It's wimpy and weak. It has no "oomph." It communicates a lack of confidence, a sense of intimidation, and general uncertainty. This is probably the most common handshake mistake, which isn't surprising since many people lack confidence, are intimidated by others, and are generally uncertain. On one hand (pardon the pun), this uncertainty could be the case. On the other hand, a floppy fish could indicate that someone is lazy or doesn't care about the introduction being made. Thus, it could also be called the "I-have-to-but-don't-want-to" handshake.

To overcome the floppy fish, just buck up and bring some life to your handshake. Keep your wrist strong. The solution may be as simple as just realizing the importance of this form of communication. At the very least, even if you're crumbling inside from nervousness, offering a solid handshake won't make it so obvious to the person you are greeting.

## THE CHURCH-LADY HANDSHAKE

During this shake the person adds an extra hand to the mix and covers the top or side of the shaking hands. This is tricky to analyze. In some cases, it conveys sympathy and can create a deeper bond between people. For instance, this handshake is quite commonly used when meeting grieving family members in a receiving line at a funeral home. In this case, the handshake shows genuine concern and support.

However, if this handshake is used in a boardroom situation or during a business function when greeting another professional, it can be seen as an intimidation technique or construed as inappropriate touching. It's taking liberties to touch the top or side of another's hand. This handshake should be reserved for close friends and associates in situations where you're actually showing sympathy and for church ladies.

## THE SOAKER HANDSHAKE

It's never comfortable to receive a wet handshake. Usually, this problem is caused when you hold a cold drink glass, your hands sweat, or you don't dry your hands completely after visiting the facilities.

To keep your hand dry, hold your drink in your left hand at cocktail receptions. If your hands sweat a lot, keep a napkin in your right-hand pocket so you can inconspicuously dry the hand you shake with before you use it for that purpose. If you don't have a pocket, keep a napkin cupped in your hand and switch the napkin to your left one just before you shake someone's hand. Take an extra moment to ensure your hands are completely dry after washing them.

## THE BONE-CRUSHER HANDSHAKE

We've all been on the receiving end of one of these handshakes. There is a fine line between a solid grip and a painful squeeze. If you happen to notice people flinch when you shake hands with them or if you regularly find yourself in a testosterone-induced shaking battle, you are probably using too strong a grip. It could mean you're extra strong or you're trying to exhibit power. Bone crushers, please lighten your grip.

To save yourself from the pain of a bone crusher, simply split your "peace" fingers and place them on the crusher's wrist rather than cupping your fingers around the crusher's hand. It will keep your bones from grinding together. (Call it lessons learned thanks to an older brother.)

## THE FINGER-LICKER HANDSHAKE

The completely unacceptable finger-licker shake happens far too often. It occurs when a person eating hors d'oeuvres at a cocktail party is kind enough to clean crumbs or grease from his fingers by licking all of them before shaking your hand. Don't laugh—yes, you may squirm—but this habit does exist. It's awkward to see a freshly licked hand coming toward you for a handshake. That's why we have napkins.

## TEST YOUR HANDSHAKE

Not sure if you have a good handshake? Watch others' facial expressions when they shake your hand. Does it change? Do they look disappointed?

Ask a friend to test your handshake. The best handshake happens when you are testing because you're cognizant of how a handshake should be. Use this opportunity to consciously improve your grip.

You really want to know if you have a strong handshake when you're meeting new contacts. Therefore, it's a good idea to ask your friend to test you in a business setting when you're not thinking about being tested. That handshake is the one that counts and will elicit real feedback.

Recently I introduced two colleagues to each other. They shook hands, said hello, and we were on our way. Afterward, my friend commented on the "floppy-fish" handshake she had just received.

The next time I saw my "floppy-fish" contact was during a training session. When I talked about appropriate handshakes, I tested this person's handshake in front of the crowd—it was a perfect grip. When he wasn't paying attention to his handshake, it was a total flop.

## HUGS AND KISSES

Hugs imply a sense of familiarity and thus should be kept for close friends and colleagues. To avoid a hug, simply offer your hand for a handshake instead. Hugs used as a greeting don't require tight or prolonged squeezes. Before going in for a hug, be sure the relationship you have with the other individual elicits one.

Offering one, two, or three "cheeky-air-kisses" is not technically a North American custom. It can make some feel uncomfortable and can be awkward, especially for those who don't wish to get up close and personal. To avoid the air kisses, simply extend your hand for the handshake and lock your elbow to keep your greeting partner at an acceptable distance.

# 29

## Name Tags

You don't wear a name tag so people know what to call you; it's worn so people know who you are. Names tags should include your first and last names plus your company name, all printed clearly. The power of a name tag is generally underestimated. A name tag is a cheat note posted on your chest for the benefit of others.

Considering the difficulty people have remembering names, using name tags properly can make it easier for people to figure out who you are and put you into context.

Placement of the name tag is as helpful as the information on it. Even though it's more awkward to get it there, the name tag should be placed on your right shoulder. Right-handed people tend to put their name tag on their left side because when the right elbow is bent, it naturally aligns to the left side, making it easier to stick it there. Name tags are ideally placed near your right shoulder, approximately three finger widths down from your collar bone. This allows people to read it with their peripheral vision as they maintain eye contact during the handshake and conversation.

### A name tag is a cheat note on your chest for others.

To help you remember, simply pretend that you are shaking someone's hand. Your right shoulder naturally falls forward. A name tag placed high on the right shoulder allows a person to look you in the eye and read your name at the same time.

There is one placement mistake that can cause uncomfortable moments. That's when a woman places her name tag too low on her chest. Ladies, a name tag is not a nipple guard. It's not appropriate to stick your name tag on your breast. Those who are well-endowed should err on the side of caution and place a name tag even higher on the shoulder.

When conference planners opt to use name tags that hang around your neck, simply tie a knot in the lanyard to shorten the length of the string to make it easier for people to read. If left at full string length, these name tags are next to impossible to read without leaning down and gazing at a person's navel. Conference planners should provide shorter strings to solve this problem for their attendees and, thankfully, I've noticed over the years this has been the trend.

At conferences, name tags hung on lanyards often double as carrying cases for hotel room keys, business cards, meal tickets, and conference agendas. Don't cover your name with these items; instead put them in the holder behind the actual name tag so your name remains visible.

Name tags are not effective when they are stuck to ties, belts, or purses. If you need to protect your jacket's fabric, consider a magnetic name tag.

A corporate name tag is okay, provided the information is legible from a distance. Large, bold letters with high contrast between the background and lettering will maximize the benefits of a professionally made name tag. Some companies insist on using name tags with the logo to capitalize on the branding opportunity.

Here's a name tag trick I learned from an associate. If, at the last minute, you are unable to attend a function, ask a colleague to remove your name tag from the reception table. By removing it, others registering won't see that you are a no-show.

# 30

## Remembering Names

HAVE YOU EVER FORGOTTEN a name? Ever been caught off guard because you were supposed to introduce two acquaintances, but you've totally blanked? Of course you have—you're human. Forgetting names is a fact of life, yet for something that happens so routinely, it causes a lot of anxiety.

It's no wonder. To an individual, his or her name is very personal and hearing it spoken is like music to his or her ears. It can make a person feel important—or unimportant—when it's his or her name that's been remembered—or forgotten. It can also make you feel like a real horse's you-know-what when you're the one who has forgotten someone's name.

Relax. Beating yourself up for being inept at remembering names is not going to make it any easier and it will likely perpetuate the problem. To alleviate pressure, the first thing to do is to accept that forgetting names happens, even for those who are usually good at remembering them.

### Forgetting names is a fact of life, yet it causes a lot of anxiety.

In fact, I've noticed as my mind sifts through the thousands of names circling around in my head that I'll second-guess myself and play it safe by not using names at all until I am sure. This is probably a reaction from every now and again getting a name wrong when I thought I was right.

Not long ago a gentleman came over to me at a formal business function. I was certain he was a long-lost contact I hadn't seen in a year. Unfortunately, he just looked like my long-lost contact and was actually a partner in a firm I was hoping would contract my training services.

I not only called him by the wrong name but I also started a conversation with him to find out what he'd been doing the last year or so.

Mr. Partner was extremely gracious and didn't draw attention to my mistake. When another individual joined our conversation, even before I had a chance to introduce him incorrectly, he simply offered his hand and gave his proper name—what a classy guy.

I immediately admitted my mistake and apologized quietly while others in the group entered into conversation around us. Turns out, he was coming to tell me that he and his business partners had decided to hire me and they'd be in touch with me soon. Talk about putting my foot into my mouth, but what could I do after the fact? To lighten the situation I joked that I would teach his associates some name-recollection techniques that actually work.

These bumps on the road of networking are bound to happen. Put them into perspective and understand that it's not the end of the world when they occur.

Remembering names is a worthwhile skill to learn. It's amazing how impressed people are when you remember their names. What a compliment you are giving them.

When I wrote the "People You Know" column for the *London Free Press*, it was my job to remember hundreds of people and their names. Comments were regularly made about my ability to remember people, not just their names, but information about them as well. Now that my job no longer requires this skill, I find it more difficult to remember names. It just goes to prove that the brain will remember what we train it to remember.

## To remember names: Shift, Listen, Solidify, and Think.

There are four keys to remembering names: Shift, Listen, Solidify, and Think.

## SHIFT

To learn how to remember names we must first understand why we forget them. Remembering names is difficult because our brain filters information we don't see as relevant. When we meet a new contact, as we have thousands of times in the past, our brain doesn't have a reason to keep the name front and center until we decide this person is important in our lives.

By shifting our thinking to understand that our brain is powerful and can remember if we make a point of it, we can start to see an improvement.

You'd remember the name of a prospect as you were walking into a sales meeting, wouldn't you? That's because your brain has placed a different level of importance on the prospect's name than it does on the random person you're meeting at a business event.

Even if you listen to the name and hear it correctly, it's easy to forget because it has no context in your life. Without anchoring it to anything that is meaningful, your brain won't register the name as important information worth remembering.

If, however, you make a conscientious effort to want to know who people are, you are more likely to remember names. Every time you meet someone, consider that person as your next client or next best friend. That will give your mind a reason to anchor the information.

## LISTEN

The challenge exists because when you meet a new contact, your mind is too busy thinking about what you're going to say next, worrying about the impression you're making, or daydreaming about items on your to-do list. With all of this mind clutter, it's easy to miss the most important part of an introduction: learning the name of the person you are meeting.

So the second step to remembering names is to focus on the task at hand and actually listen carefully to the name when it's given to you.

During the introduction I listen rather than worrying about what I'm going to say next or looking to see who else I can meet. I focus solely on the person I am meeting. Listening is much easier to do if you genuinely want to meet new people and care about what they have to say.

## SOLIDIFY

Next, I take a mental snapshot of the person to solidify the name and the image in my conscious mind (and probably in my subconscious mind, but I can't tell you that for sure because it's subconscious).

My mental snapshot includes a bit about the location where we're meeting and the person's name tag, which is why I'm a huge believer in the importance of name tags. They add a visual reminder of the name, so I am sure to use it as well as the audio message. This image is the reason I can run into a person six months later and often pinpoint when and where we met. If we had a good chat or shared a laugh, I can usually remember a little about the person.

As they say, a picture is worth a thousand words. With a little practice and specific intent, solidifying freeze-framed mental snapshots in your mind will give you something to recall when you see this person again. Hopefully, at the very least, this picture will be worth two words: the person's first and last names.

## THINK

The most important strategy to remembering names is to think. After meeting people, I reflect on our conversations. What did we talk about? Who were they? What do they do? What did I like about them? How did we connect? Who introduced us? I don't spend hours obsessing over everyone I meet, but just a moment of conscious awareness after a conversation seems to pay dividends in the long run to winning the name game.

If I missed a name during an introduction, I look and listen for clues. In group discussions someone will usually reference a person's name, which is a great reminder. I read name tags and business cards. I ask mutual contacts, "Who is that again?" I read program books and event agendas to look for names of committee members, key volunteers, and sponsors. I gather all the information I can and connect the dots.

# 31

# Forgetting Names

## *When Your Name Has Been Forgotten*

Is IT POSSIBLE? Could someone really have the nerve to forget your name? Let me ask you this: If you've forgotten names, isn't it safe to assume that others may forget your name?

Do not take offense when someone forgets your name. Memory recall isn't always the sharpest and people have a lot on their minds. It's arrogant to think that remembering your name is a top priority on a contact's to-do list, particularly when you've only met a few times.

It takes six to eight times of meeting someone casually before a person "gets" who you are and vice versa. Have you ever been sitting in a committee meeting and after several months of being on the same committee with someone, you look across the table, have that moment of clarity, and say to yourself, "Oh yeah, hey, I know that person"?

### Do not take offense when someone forgets your name.

Accept that others have distractions, problems, and priorities in their lives. Do whatever you can to make it easy for people to know who you are, what you do, and what you have to offer. The easier you make it for someone to remember your name, the more likely he or she is to remember it.

When saying hello to a casual contact, offer your first and last name again. This will eliminate the name-game pressure. Your effort to make others comfortable will encourage them to offer their name as well. A person who says "Of course I know your name" could secretly be thrilled that you gave a kind reminder.

If you find yourself in a group situation and your contact has not introduced you, he may have forgotten someone in the group's name (maybe yours). Simply extend your hand to others and introduce yourself to add comfort to a potentially uncomfortable moment.

To be extra considerate, add a one-line anecdote to explain your connection to the mutual contact. Your hint could ease the situation. For example, say "Hi, I'm so-and-so. I just joined Bob's Rotary Club about a month ago." Immediately Bob will clue in to who you are and the conversation can flow from there.

Unfortunately, people will routinely give their first name only during introductions. Give your first and last name up front to make it easier for people to put you into context and introduce you to their contacts. Often it's the inclusion of the last name that will trigger an association that can lead to a conversation or discovery of a mutual friend.

## WHEN YOU FORGET SOMEONE'S NAME

When you're the person who has forgotten someone's name you may just need time for your memory to kick into gear, so continue the conversation and hope for a clue.

It's also acceptable to be honest, especially with someone you know you've only met once or twice. You could simply say "I'm trying to remember where we first met" or "Forgive me, my brain's obviously not working up to snuff. What is your name again?" Be sure to listen when the name is repeated so you remember it next time. Return the favor by offering your name, as well, to save others from having to ask.

If you've forgotten a name and you are required to introduce two people, simply ask, "Have you two met?" Naturally, the two will introduce themselves. That's when you listen to hear their names again.

# 32

# Dining Etiquette

DINING ETIQUETTE IS A lost art form. Nothing reminds me of this more than sitting at a business function and watching people navigate formal and even informal dinner tables. Dining etiquette is about being considerate to your tablemates. The basics are easy to learn. When you don't know what to do, simply ask yourself, "What is the considerate option?"

For example, it's inconsiderate to chew with your mouth open or to talk with food in your mouth. It's inconsiderate to lick your fingers, especially when you are about to shake someone's hand. It's inconsiderate to shovel food into your mouth or to focus so much on food that you ignore others at the table. It's inconsiderate to put your dirty napkin on the table for others to see while they are still eating. It's inconsiderate to monopolize the conversation with topics that make people feel uncomfortable. You get the picture.

## Not sure? Ask yourself: What's the considerate option?

## PLACE SETTINGS

Solids are on the left, liquids on the right. That means your bread plate is on the left side beside your forks, and your drinking glasses are on the right side above the knife and spoons. To make this easy to remember, make the "OK" sign with your fingers with both hands. Your left hand forms the letter *b* for *bread* and your right forms a *d* for *drinks*. As the first person to sit at the table, this trick will help you start the plates and glasses correctly.

If the table settings have been started incorrectly and you are forced to use the wrong bread plate and drink glasses, be considerate by not drawing attention to the situation. This could embarrass the person who started using the settings incorrectly. You can, however, simply move the available bread plate to the proper side and once you've taken a sip from your glass, you can place it on the right side, which happens to be on the right side.

## NAPKINS

Once seated, immediately place your napkin on your lap. Do not tuck it into your shirt to use it as a bib. To avoid splashing on your clothes, eat carefully and at a comfortable pace.

When you place the napkin on your lap, fold the furthest few inches of the napkin over on itself. This way, you can use that inside edge of the napkin to dab your lips. When you place it back on your lap, fold the soiled end back over on itself so you will protect your clothing and hide the mess.

Please do not lick your fingers; that's why you have a napkin. Never use your napkin as a tissue to blow your nose at the table.

If you need to leave during the meal, say a soft "Excuse me" to those on either side of you, and then leave your napkin on your chair, not on the table. When you leave at the end of the meal, you can put your napkin, folded loosely, on the table to let the server know you are not returning.

## USING SILVERWARE IN NORTH AMERICA

Choose silverware from the outside first and work your way in toward the plate. Utensils placed horizontally across the top of your place setting are for coffee and dessert. Technically, you should have new silverware for each course. If the server insists you keep your silverware, place it on your bread plate, not back on the tablecloth, because it's inconsiderate to soil the tablecloth with your utensils. Don't point or gesture with your silverware. Never lick your knife. Cut one piece of food at a time: we are not children.

Although it is elegant to use the Continental eating style that would be appropriate and required in European culture, the North American eating style is acceptable while on this continent. Just choose which is most comfortable for you and do it gracefully.

## North American Style

When cutting food, the fork should be held in your left hand and the knife in your right. To take a bite of food, lay your knife on the top-right edge of your plate and transfer your fork to your right hand. Bring the food to your mouth with fork tines facing upward.

## Continental Style

This practice is considered more formal and is customary in other parts of the world. Rather than changing hands to cut and eat, the fork and knife remain in the same hand throughout the meal. The knife is in your right hand and your fork is kept in your left, positioned with tines facing down.

## CIRCULATING ITEMS

It is your responsibility to notice and begin to circulate items directly in front of you. Pass items to the right; however, offer the bread to your left, then choose your own piece from the basket before passing it to the right. Since many people are not aware of this proper procedure, you may find that when you offer the bread to the person on your left, they'll actually take the basket from you and send it around the table the wrong way. Instead of instigating a tug-of-war with the bread basket to correct it, just let it go. Pass salt and pepper as a set, even if only one is requested.

## BREAD AND BUTTER

The bread plate is on your left side. Using the knife provided on the butter dish or using your personal butter knife provided on your bread plate, scoop butter directly from the dish to your bread plate—not directly to your bread. Break a piece of bread, butter it (one piece at a time), and eat it.

Eat everything that goes toward your mouth in one bite. Food that goes up to your mouth does not go back down to your plate. Watching a person make a butter sandwich and proceed to gnaw off a hunk of bread and put the rest down is not an enjoyable, albeit a frequent, occurrence.

## EATING SOUP

Draw the spoon away from you to fill it with soup. Quietly sip the soup from the side of the spoon. Tilt the bowl away from you to get the last drops. Do not sip directly from the bowl.

To eliminate soup drips falling from the bottom of your spoon, simply dip the under edge of your spoon into the top of the soup rather than wiping it on the edge of your bowl. Yes, remarkably, this works. When finished eating the soup, rest the spoon on the plate below the bowl. If there is no plate, you can leave the spoon in the bowl.

## SALAD

The chef should prepare salad in bite-size pieces. However, if the pieces of salad are too large to eat, use the edge of your salad fork to cut them into smaller pieces. As a last resort, use your dinner knife to cut the lettuce, but that means you will need a new knife for your main course if one has not been provided. If you have to keep your soiled knife, set it on your bread plate.

## CONCLUSION OF MEAL

In North America, place utensils at the 4:20 position to signal that you are finished your meal. The fork tines face up and the knife blade should face the fork. This will protect the server from accidentally being cut should the knife slide. Again, it's about being considerate.

It is rude to stack your plates, push them away, or hand them to the server at formal dinners. Place your loosely folded napkin, soiled side down and hidden, on the table just as you stand to leave, not before.

## GENERAL MANNERS

Stand at attention if the national anthem is played. Be quiet and respectful during grace, if it is said. Use the water glass when toasting the Queen. Do not clink glasses during a toast. Raise your glass, make eye contact with your tablemates, and nod your head slightly. After the toast is completed, take a sip of the liquid to complete the ritual.

The meal officially begins when the host takes the first bite. Wait for all guests to be seated and served before you begin to eat.

Keep the pace of your tablemates as you eat.

Don't talk while someone is speaking from the microphone; it is inconsiderate and can make it difficult for a speaker to concentrate. Regardless of how quiet you think you are whispering, you'll never be quiet enough to avoid irritating those around you who are trying to listen.

Don't go to an event hungry. It will make it easier for you to focus on the people rather than the food. Buffets at business functions are not to be treated the same as all-you-can-eat buffets at restaurants. Take your fair share, but not so much that you look greedy.

Keep your elbows off the table until the dinner plates have been removed.

Eat quietly. Avoid smacking sounds or hitting your teeth with your silverware. The irritation of sharing a meal with a person who constantly grinds his fork to his teeth is equivalent to hearing fingernails scratching on a chalkboard.

When eating hors d'oeuvres, stand close to a table so you can rest your glass and eat comfortably. When plates are not available, only take one hors d'oeuvre at a time.

Make sure that all the words you say at a dinner table or in a buffet line are appropriate. Health issues, body functions, accidents, etc., are not welcome subjects for mealtime.

# 33

## Objectives for Attending Events

THE MAIN REASON YOU GO to business functions is to meet people and reconnect with contacts—not to talk with your colleagues and friends. Save those personal conversations for personal time.

Events are not the time to sell your product or pitch your latest idea, nor are they where the bulk of your relationships will be made. Group settings are for introductions, small chat, and light business talk. They are a great place to identify connections so you can follow up outside the event, which is where the strong business relationships are built.

When I say *event* or *function* I mean anything that is a formalized activity with potential for interaction with people. Some examples are a charity gala, a speaker's series, a lunch and learn, or a breakfast club.

### Group settings are for introductions, small chat, and light business talk.

The best part about business events is that they collect people with a common denominator for you. Depending on the function, the common thread will change, but basically, others are there to meet new people and reconnect with current contacts too. Your job is to attend and connect with them. If you don't, chances are your competition will.

Some events are more effective for networking than others, as we'll explore in the Fourth Pillar, but as a general rule, if you show up consistently and persistently in areas where your target market is gathered, and you present a welcoming, genuine, professional image, you can't help but build a profitable network.

You should have a reason for attending each event. Sometimes that reason is just for fun, but when it comes to profitable networking we want to combine enjoyable outings with results. The worst reason to go to an event is because you feel you should. The "shoulds" in life will drive you crazy.

When you walk in with the attitude that you are at this event to find the people with whom you connect enough that you want to connect again, then you'll send a good vibe and be open to making great connections.

# 34

## Calculating the Return on Investment for Events

HAVE YOU EVER CALCULATED what it truly costs you to attend an event?

As a rough estimate, take your hourly rate (which may be different from your hourly wage) and multiply it by the number of hours needed for the event. Add the ticket price, any extra costs such as drink tickets and auction prizes, expenses incurred getting to the function, and the investment needed to dress for the event and you have calculated a base amount needed for your attendance. Don't forget to consider the intangible costs inherent in being away from your office or your family.

As you can imagine, each event can get pricey. Don't get me wrong; this math exercise is not to give you an excuse to avoid networking events, but rather, it's a wake-up call so that when you do go to events you are mindful to make them worthwhile.

### What does it cost you to attend an event?

The reality is if you want to build a profitable network, then you have to go where there are people. The potentially high cost associated with networking is the exact reason why you must make good business decisions when it comes to attending or sending employees to events.

It's simply impossible to calculate the true return on your time invested when networking. In my case, I owe my entire career to the chain of events that started with a single Saturday morning reception.

What price tag would you put on meeting your biggest client, finding your best friend, or landing your dream job? There may be tangible financial benefits that can make such connections measurable but the quality of life and the intangibles that come from having the ultimate network are priceless.

It's equally impossible to put a figure on what it costs you to *not* network. How can you calculate what you don't know could happen? Had I chosen to stay in bed that Saturday morning, my life's path would arguably be quite different. Sure, I would have eventually found success, but I doubt my path would have been the same or that I would have accomplished so much in so little time.

What is the opportunity cost for continuing to struggle to meet new people or reach your sales targets? The time spent cold calling and advertising to attract new clients could be better spent building your network and setting the foundation for long-term success.

Networking naysayers show up once or twice, don't meet any new clients, and make a judgment call that all networking events are a waste of time based on inefficient efforts. They don't give the natural processes of networking and relationship building the chance they deserve.

Events, when used properly, can be a gold mine for your business-networking efforts, yet so few professionals really take advantage of the opportunity to its fullest.

It boggles my mind how companies will spend $1,500 to buy a table at a business or charity event and allow their executives, sales reps, and staff to sit together and spend all night talking. They spend all this money so their employees can move their water cooler conversation of the day to a very expensive round table at night. What a waste of company resources. Variations of this ineffective approach to attending events happen all the time.

Consider the impact had those same employees spent the night talking with current and potential clients and reconnecting with contacts. At the very least, cut the number from the company in half and invite guests to join the table instead. Then, half of the faces in the group are potential business opportunities for the company.

If you've ever left an event and thought to yourself, "Okay, there are five wasted hours of my life I will never get back," then you're not alone. Unless you are a natural-born schmoozer, business functions seem intimidating and difficult to navigate to make them worthwhile.

The good news is that you can make attending events valuable. They are just one part of the networking process, but they can be catalysts for your success, as they were for mine. It just takes some perspective, preparation, and practice. Tackle one idea at a time and build momentum until networking becomes second nature.

Natural-born networkers should stick with what's already working for them. Incorporate your personality with the mechanics of working your way through a crowd. Use the tips that follow to tweak your talents and to ensure you maximize opportunities to achieve success.

It's tough to measure networking results because a relationship's real value won't be realized immediately. It can take a lifetime to really understand the impact of any one person on your professional career. Therefore, we need to set measurable benchmarks to ensure you are on track.

## It can take a lifetime to understand the impact of any one person on your professional career.

Different types of events can be measured differently. A breakfast event with your business referral group can be measured in referrals gained. The value can further be calculated by the revenue from those referrals and subsequent spin-off business.

The rewards from other events aren't quite as obvious. A general networking event with a cross-section of professionals from your community can lead to a low number of target-market contacts, but can lead to mentoring relationships, charitable alignments, and personal fulfillment, all of which have significant long-term value. Goodwill and increased brand awareness, while difficult to pinpoint, can't be understated.

Industry-specific, target market–rich events should give you 5 to 10 quality contacts that require follow-up. From them, at least 1 should materialize as a client, and 1 or 2 as ongoing prospects. Inevitably 2 or 3 will amount to no further action.

Some events are just about you having fun. Then, you can measure the good time you had rather than the contacts gained. There is value in recharging our batteries.

## Some events are just about having fun. There is value in recharging our batteries.

The easiest way to measure your event-going success is to set benchmarks by choosing a reasonable number of quality contacts from each event to add to your network. Five is a good, easy number. If you're not as outgoing or eager to meet new people, then one new contact per event may suit your fancy. Only you will know how you define "quality contact." At minimum, these five new contacts are people with whom you've connected, shared a solid conversation, and determined that follow-up is required.

There is also value in reconnecting with current contacts and this should be included in any event-going-success calculations. If I'm trying to secure a contract and the process has stalled, I'll purposely run into a decision maker in a social setting so I can get back on his or her radar screen and give a gentle nudge for a phone call or meeting.

When you think there is a business opportunity and a reason to connect with a senior-level person, simply running into that decision maker every month for an entire year is not ideal. At some point, you have to move the conversation away from the casual encounters and get to the table. If there is no immediate need for your services, then just constantly running into each other is a great strategy to stay on their radar screen. During those encounters be sure you are creating a sense of familiarity and are saying enough about your work that they will understand who you are, what you do, and what you have to offer.

If this is happening a lot, you may find you're spinning your wheels having a lot of nice conversations, but not seeing the desired results. After three encounters in event settings with someone who is a prospect, you need to aim for a one-on-one follow-up session to move the relationship or sales process forward. Otherwise you could end up having them stay in prospect purgatory for too long. More on that in the Fourth Pillar.

The real return on investment from networking will show in the long run. Keeping year-over-year stats on how many people are part of your active network and, of them, how many are materializing as new business leads can be helpful for those who have to answer to senior executives and justify networking budgets.

For the rest of us, just ask yourself if you're feeling more connected and look at your bottom line. If it's growing more easily than it was in the past then you're on the right profitable networking track.

# 35

## Networking Effectively with Spouses, Friends, and Work Colleagues

YOUR DECISION TO PROACTIVELY build your business network means some of your habits will have to change. Talking all night with your best friend at business functions or treating business functions as dates with your spouse will not garner the results you want.

Networking buddies who enable you to network and vice versa are gems to find. Done correctly, the two of you can increase your confidence because you always have each other to return to, but not for long, if you're left on your own. You can also double the number of contacts you meet by splitting up and meeting different people. If one of you finds an ideal quality contact for the other, you can make a point of introducing the two of you.

The right networking companion can act as your cheerleader by sharing appropriate personal highlights and success stories to give you credibility. These would be tacky for you to share during an introduction. Later in the relationship, once the dialogue is more free-flowing, you can share your own successes, but at the beginning of a relationship it's more effective to let someone else toot your horn. It's sort of like when you were younger, if you had a mom who was over the top in sharing your successes, she would introduce you to someone and announce that you just won an award at school. It's okay if she said it, but if you said "Hi, I'm Allison and I just won the business award," people would look at you sideways and think you were arrogant. Same principle applies. It helps if you both know each other's messaging and target markets before the event.

The perfect networking companion is someone who shares your networking goals, is not your direct competition, supports you, recognizes ideal prospects for you, and is most happy to hold you accountable to follow up.

## The perfect networking companion is someone who shares your networking goals and is not your competition.

Having a networking buddy doesn't always run that smoothly. Watch the level of conversation you have with each other. It's easy for work colleagues to gossip about office politics, best friends to get catty, and spouses to have conversations that are better left for home.

To network effectively as a team, you'll have to detach from one another's hip when at functions. "Birds of a feather flock together," so be sure your networking buddy is up to speed on business etiquette and is projecting a professional image that you're happy to reflect on you as well. Ask your friend for feedback on how you present yourself and do the same for him or her.

Having conversations as a duo with new contacts can limit your ability to grow your own personal brand. Therefore, it is important to separate. Even business partners are encouraged to network independently, showing people that you have two competent business owners who come together to make a good team rather than two people who are inseparable.

Thankfully, because there isn't the same emotional investment, it's much easier to explain to a work colleague the importance of separating to network than it is to tell the same thing to a spouse or a date.

Spouses may need to shift their attitudes and expectations to support you as you build your profitable network just as you may need to shift how you communicate about your networking efforts. Spouses should complement what you're doing, not cause you undue stress at business functions. Be sure your significant other understands what you're trying to accomplish, that it won't happen overnight, and that the commitment required to be successful will be intense. To minimize last-minute stress, it's helpful to keep your spouse in the loop and schedule events in advance.

When you attend an event on behalf of your company, you are on your company's time. Your spouse should be aware of your work expectations in advance and should allow you the freedom to mingle in a professional manner. Remember, business functions are not dates. It can cause friction if one of you is completely uncomfortable networking and the other likes to roam the room.

If you do take your spouse, remember to treat each other with respect. Business functions are not the time to highlight and solve your spouse's inadequacies.

## Business functions are not the time to highlight and solve your spouse's inadequacies.

The time to discuss these differences is *before* the event, not *during* it. It's uncomfortable for everyone within ear shot to listen to a couple argue about how much time he spent talking with another woman, how one of the two was left alone too long or to watch the evil eye flash between them.

If your spouse lacks business savvy and dining etiquette, work with him or her outside the function in a constructive way, but when you're in public, just let it go. Drawing attention to your spouse's deficiencies will just help others see them.

I'll never forget sitting by a couple at a black-tie gala. Obviously, the formal environment was not the husband's forte and the wife wouldn't let him forget it. Every time he opened his mouth to speak, she nudged him under the table. A nudge we could all feel. We could also feel his embarrassment. By trying to keep him in line, she drew attention to his shortcomings and turned what could have been a fun night into an uncomfortable situation for everyone at the table.

It's a rare couple who can complement each other's networking efforts. I'm privileged to know several and it's easy to see the difference between those who move in business circles well as a couple and those who don't.

If your spouse isn't into it, doesn't "get it," or you feel he or she cramps your style, it's best (and easiest) to leave him or her at home, attend your function solo, then spend quality time with your partner afterward. When your spouse does go with you, just go with the flow. What we see in our loved ones is not the same as what others see. Their long-winded stories may annoy you, but the new contact may sincerely enjoy the details in the story. It's important to give them the room to be themselves. After all, they are adults.

# 36

# Before an Event

WOULD YOU WALK INTO a meeting with a client unprepared? Of course not. You would risk looking unorganized, while wasting time for both of you. Preparation for a business function should be given the same respect.

Regardless of the time of day or how you choose to fill your hours, the value of your time remains constant. An hour spent in a boardroom costs you the same amount as an hour spent at a function. Why wouldn't you give the same consideration to business functions as you do to time spent in company meetings? When you network, you are engaging in an equally important business activity.

This doesn't mean that for every function you'll have to write a full report, create an agenda, consider objectives, and analyze anticipated outcomes. However, you should at least formulate some thoughts as to the event's purpose and have a game plan for what you're going to do when you're there.

## Before you go, determine your intention for attending the event and do your pre-event homework.

Before you go to a function, determine your intention for attending the event and do your pre-event homework. Visit the organization's website. Who is on the board? Who is sponsoring the event? Is anyone being honored? Who will likely attend? Who is the host? Why are you going? What is your intention? How does this event fit with your focus board? (See Chapter 63: Finding Your Focus.) What is the dress code? Who do you hope to meet? What is the purpose of the event?

Check the agenda. When is the best time to arrive? When your time is limited, the priority for your attendance should be the informal portion of any event. That's when guests mingle and you can connect with the greatest number of people. Arriving just in time to hear the speaker or to sit for dinner doesn't allow you much opportunity to network.

When you have a reason to go to a function, you will know when you can leave. You don't always have to stay for the entire event. If you meet your objectives early, you can adjust your departure time accordingly.

This targeted approach for maximizing your attendance at events is handy when your to-do list is overloaded and you want to go home to your family. Don't make a big deal about sneaking out early; just do what you came to do and quietly excuse yourself.

Before you enter an event, take a mental note of your attitude and confidence level. If your mood is projecting anything less than a warm, welcoming, professional image, then have a talk with yourself, adjust your mood, and get your act together. Find your smile before you see someone else's face at the event.

There are days when you may not feel like going to another event or speaking with another person. That's natural. I'll admit to having those days. But, if you're committed to building your profitable network, you can't sit at home watching television and eating popcorn, hoping people will "get" who you are. Ironically, it's usually the events that you attend when you don't feel like attending that prove to be the best times.

## To shift your attitude, focus on others.

A good way to shift your attitude is to focus on others. Helping and connecting other people always brings a warm, fuzzy feeling to the potentially harsh reality of business. By focusing on others you can forget about the crummy experiences that happened earlier in your day and enjoy the company of the people in the room.

If you're not feeling confident, review the personal adjective list you created in the Personal Brand section, pages 44–45. Focus on the bigger picture and your long-term objectives. Envision how much easier life will be with a profitable network.

Before each event, regardless of your mood, review the definition of business networking and set realistic expectations. Be aware of your own agenda, then forget it. Yes, you want to connect with the people you came to meet, but it's a balancing act between accomplishing your goals and taking your eyes off yourself so you can genuinely connect with others. Have a purpose, but don't be calculating.

Remind yourself that it is your responsibility to make it easy for people to know who you are, what you do, and what you have to offer.

Take care of the Business of YOU before you go. Are you dressed and groomed in a professional manner? Are your clothes clean and pressed? Do they match the dress code? Dealing with the Business of YOU first will give you the confidence to stop worrying about the impression you're going to make.

Review the event notice. What do you need to take with you? For instance, do you need to take a payment, ticket, parking pass, or directions to the location?

Such a routine may seem tedious, but eventually reviewing this checklist will become automatic. Once you're all set and ready for your event, put a smile on your face, grab a stack of business cards, and be on your way.

## PRE-EVENT CHECKLIST

**Details:**

- ❏ Ticket or invitation
- ❏ Location
- ❏ Directions
- ❏ Parking pass
- ❏ Dress code
- ❏ Extra requirements: hostess gift, donation, food-drive item

**The Business of YOU:**

- ❏ Well-groomed
- ❏ Attitude adjusted
- ❏ Interested in connecting with others
- ❏ Confidence: review your list of top 20 positive qualities from Chapter 24
- ❏ Smile

**The Fundamentals**

- ❏ Business cards: inbox/outbox (see Chapter 47: Business Cards)
- ❏ Handshake: ready for firm, web-to-web grip with solid wrist
- ❏ Name tag: placed high on the right shoulder, includes first and last names, and company
- ❏ Dining etiquette: plan to be considerate of others

**The Strategy**

- ❏ Reviewed meaning and objectives for proper business networking
- ❏ Checked agenda: determined best time to go and scheduled enough time
- ❏ Determined purpose for attending
- ❏ Reviewed list of sponsors, committee members, or honorees

# 37

# Understanding Event Flow

EVERY EVENT FOLLOWS A TYPICAL FLOW. Once understood, event flow dynamics can help you choose the most advantageous time to network and thus when you should arrive and leave.

**TYPICAL EVENT FLOW**

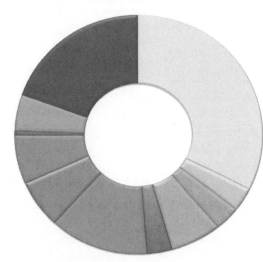

- Event Setup
- Anticipation of Arrival
- Early Birds Arrive
- Event Energy
- Call to Order
- Official Program
- Antsy People
- Completion of Program
- Bolt to the Door
- After-Conversations
- Post-Event Follow-Ups

For each event, notice the best time for you to network and adjust your arrival time accordingly. As you can see, the greatest opportunity is to get involved during the event setup and preparation phase. The least amount of opportunity to network is during the official program. Visit www.BC2BR.com for a verbal explanation of the typical event flow and how it can affect your networking results!

The chart above shows that the best time to arrive for networking isn't necessarily at the obvious time, which is often believed to be just in time for the formal program.

Busy professionals will commit to an event and expect to get there well after the official start. Arriving "fashionably late" means you'll miss prime networking opportunities and be forced to walk into a potentially intimidating crowd.

### Arriving fashionably late means you'll miss prime networking opportunities.

Arriving at the scheduled beginning gives you a greater chance that the organizers will be available for a quick chat and as people arrive they will hand you off to someone else by making an introduction. If they understand their own job as hosts, they realize their organizational work is done and now, as people arrive, their role is to facilitate a successful networking event.

It's easier to meet people at the beginning of an event. People are still warming up and getting into "networking mode." Chances are their friends have not arrived yet and event hosts will be waiting for people to fill the room. It's much less intimidating to walk into a room occupied by just a few people than to walk into a room filled with an active crowd where everyone is already engaged in conversation.

Adjust your arrival time for your next event. Instead of sneaking in at the last minute or when the bulk of the people will arrive, go early. Feel the difference in the dynamics when you do this. Was it easier to launch into conversations when there were only a few people in the room? Did you feel more confident walking into an almost empty room rather than a full room of people talking?

If you really want to get connected with a particular group, taking a leadership role and volunteering for the event is a good start because there is such a long lead time before large events come to fruition. This "in the trenches" kind of work can solidify mini-bonds into professional relationships.

You can also see from the chart there is an opportunity for networking after the event formally ends. Avoid the bolt to the door and watch who is left in the room after the mass departure is complete. The results may surprise you. Most people leave immediately at the conclusion of the formal portion of an event so it's likely you'll catch the bulk of the people by going early; however, the post-event phase is an excellent relationship-building time. There are fewer people in the room, but with less hustle and bustle you're more likely to engage in deeper conversations. It's better to stay a little longer than waste time stuck in the parking lot trying to leave with the majority.

Your schedule may not always let you arrive early and stay late, but understanding the value of doing so can help you prioritize it in your schedule. Just add the extra time on either side. If you're going to invest three hours at an event that is supposed to last three and a half hours why not try to go for the whole thing? Shift your block of time to include the portion of the event that will have the greatest return on investment.

# 38

# Arrival

SET YOUR INTENTION AND CHECK your attitude as you arrive at the function. The last time you should worry about *you* is when you enter the room. Forget your agenda, stop worrying about your overloaded to-do list, clear your mind of self-doubt, and get ready to enjoy the process.

How you behave at public events will set the foundation for your personal brand and reputation. The event begins when you arrive in the parking lot and ends when you drive away. Parking lots are excellent places to meet new people who are on the way into the same event. If you are concerned you won't know many people, it's a non-intimidating place to practice starting conversations with new contacts. Do so in a way that is friendly and doesn't seem like you're a stalker. It's best to talk with people who are obviously en route to the same place. This works easier in small towns and smaller urban centers because in large cities you may not park in the same lot, let alone drive to get there.

### The last time you should worry about *you* is when you enter the room.

Focus on the other people at the event. They'll appreciate your genuine interest in them and your selfless nature will be noticed, even if it is subtle.

To build event-going confidence, find your own routine. When you enter, pause for a moment to scan the room. Who's there? What's happening? What's the tone of the room? Where are the amenities? Who do you know? Who do you want to know?

Take care of housekeeping duties first. Register, pay your admission, affix your name tag, check table seating, and buy drink tickets. Then you are free to mingle. If you're not a fan of conversations with strangers, use the registration process to practice engaging in dialogue with new contacts. This warm-up will help you prepare to connect with known and unknown people as you circulate through the room.

After you've entered and taken a moment to scan the room, make your first move. Yes, walking into a room full of strangers can be intimidating. Relax. One day the situation will reverse itself. You'll know everyone in the room and you'll be greeting newcomers to make them feel comfortable.

Work your way to and from a determined point in the room or imagine making a figure 8 as you network your way through the crowd. Start by heading toward the middle of the most populated area. Then, mingle your way through both sides of the crowd. It will establish a sense of direction for you and encourage you to meet more people because you know you have to complete your figure 8 or get to the bar and back before dinner is called.

No need to worry if you find yourself left alone for a minute or two in between conversations or before you find your first conversation partner. Instinctively we don't want to look like the loner in the room so we beeline to the one person we know best and settle into the comfort zone for the night. By taking a breath and slowing down the entry process you may see someone else or allow time for a new contact to be made.

Rest assured, people will not point and laugh at you and think you are an unpopular loser with whom no one wants to talk. I haven't seen it happen yet. However, I have seen the look of panic on the faces of those who are left alone. It must be residual psychological effects from school playgrounds because I've not met anyone who is completely comfortable standing on his or her own in a room full of people.

However, time on your own will give you a chance to regroup and determine where you want to go next, allowing you to take a proactive approach to mingling. It will also give others a chance to approach you. Granted, if you do remain on your own for too long—like, say, for most of the event—you will look awkward and out of place.

# 39

## Mingling Formula

HAVE YOU EVER WONDERED how some people float through a room seemingly effortlessly? They appear to connect with people in a matter of seconds and then move to the next person without hesitation. It helps to know many people, but guaranteed, there was a time when that social butterfly didn't know anyone in the room.

Rarely do I go to an event now where I don't know a majority of the attendees, but that wasn't always the case. When I started my networking journey, I wouldn't have known which room to walk into, let alone who was there. At some point, a room full of strangers became a room full of contacts. Mingling made that happen.

As my company developed, I learned that mingling was a real barrier for people so I took a closer look at how one mingles effectively and voilà—my Mingling Formula was developed:

1. Initiate dialogue.
2. Create a mini-bond.
3. Exchange contact information (or at least know how to get it).
4. Move on.
5. Repeat often.

It's that simple. Once you've tackled each element, you'll be ready and able to make your way through any crowd effortlessly. Anyone who knows more than two people (his or her parents) has successfully completed the

Mingling Formula thousands of times in life. Even if you don't formalize it, the Mingling Formula is how all relationships begin.

Think about it: You meet. You start talking. You decide you like each other so you exchange contact information. Then you leave. You already practice this daily. Maybe not all elements of the Mingling Formula occur during each encounter, but variations of the formula happen routinely.

## Life has prepared you to be a master at mingling.

Have confidence that life has already prepared you to be a master at mingling. What you've lived every day of your life is the same process that will help you maximize business functions.

Step 1, initiating dialogue, happens frequently. It could be as simple as talking with the cashier when you buy something at the store or commenting on the weather when you share an elevator. Initiating dialogue does not mean you have to have a full-blown conversation.

Mingling at an event may seem more intimidating because it's a formalized business environment and there are more people with whom you can engage in the process. A crowd is no more than a bunch of individuals gathered in the same place. The fact that you are in the crowd means you already have something in common with others who are there.

As we discussed earlier, the keys to effective business networking and building confidence come from perspective, preparation, and practice. The same rules apply when engaging with new contacts and becoming a master at mingling.

- **Perspective:** Understand that others go to events to connect with people just as you do and many of them have the same fears and hesitations when it comes to talking with strangers.
- **Preparation:** Know the Mingling Formula. Have potential topics ready to discuss and your favorite conversation starters ready to go.
- **Practice:** The more you experience the Mingling Formula the easier it will become. One day, engaging in conversations with strangers at functions will be as comfortable as talking with your closest associates.

# 40

# Initiating Dialogue

THE LOGICAL BEGINNING OF EVERY relationship is conversation. Initiating dialogue is an important first step; without the onset of a conversation, how will you get to know someone?

When we were young, our parents taught us to not talk to strangers. For many, this remains imbedded in their attitudes as they set out to build a network. To build your ultimate network, you're going to have to let this rule go and start talking with people you don't know yet.

The best way to initiate dialogue is to simply make eye contact and say "Hello." Rarely will people turn away from you, provided you present a professional, confident, and inviting image. If you do, and they still snub you, that's their problem, not yours. When you use this approach, prepare to lead the conversation somewhere. It's uncomfortable to stop a conversation after hello.

**The best way to initiate dialogue is to simply make eye contact and say "Hello."**

When looking for a conversation partner in a crowded room there are three likely scenarios that make it easy to initiate dialogue:

1. Fun, inviting groups
2. White-knuckled loners who look uncomfortable and will welcome your attempt to initiate dialogue
3. Familiar faces

When it comes to initiating dialogue, accept that for the most part, conversation openers will not be that original or exciting. It's the formality of the beginning of any relationship. True connections develop thanks to the direction of the dialogue after it's been initiated.

Use your surroundings to strike up a conversation. Situational dialogue offers common ground and can lead to laughs and further conversation. Take notice of what's happening around you, as this is natural ammunition for great conversations.

It helps to have some key questions and conversation starters ready to use in those potentially uncomfortable first few moments after an introduction. Having several opening lines and topics on the tip of your tongue will give you confidence and clear your head when being introduced to new contacts. This should make it easier to listen and subsequently to remember a person's name.

As a note of caution, preparation is important, but it's equally important to be natural and act in the moment. If you sound like a robot and ask the same question every time you meet someone new or ask questions that don't have a natural flow that fits the environment, you run the risk of sounding contrived and phony. Having a variety of starters is helpful to make initiating dialogue easier over time.

Here are some suggested open-ended questions that can get conversations flowing:

- How do you two know each other?
- What's your connection to this event?
- What keeps you busy when you're not at functions like this?
- How are you involved with this organization?
- How did you find out about tonight?

The answers to these questions will lead to more in-depth dialogue. Avoid using anything that is too far-fetched. I've heard some people ask questions such as "If you were a fruit, what fruit would you be?" or "Where's the one place in the world you'd prefer to be?"

Sure, the answers may be revealing, but it's tough to be taken seriously as a businessperson when asking abstract questions. Some appreciate originality, but this type of probing will stretch people out of their comfort zones before a mini-bond has been established.

Uncomfortable silence often occurs when two people are introduced by a third party and neither offers any conversational tidbit to get the ball rolling after the handshakes. It goes something like this: "Nice to meet you." "Yes, nice to meet you too." Then both look back to the introducer for a prolonged session of dead air.

More than once, I've introduced two people and after the handshakes, one of the contacts just walks away. I have one associate who does this frequently. When I asked her about the reason behind the "meet-and-run" pattern, her response was "I don't want to interrupt or impose on you and your contacts." This is likely the reason many people don't stick around to engage in conversation after casual introductions.

I recall one particularly uncomfortable situation when a contact entered a conversation to speak with me. After I introduced her to the person I had been talking with, she shook her hand and then vanished! We were both left feeling bewildered. To my original conversation partner, her abrupt exit was insulting.

For me, I was annoyed and confused as to why my contact interrupted a conversation already in progress and then purposely or accidentally insulted my associate because she had no intention of continuing the communication with us.

This rude behavior gives the impression that "I'm too good to talk to you" and makes people feel insulted and snubbed—even if it's unintentional.

Initiating dialogue is much easier when you project an image that communicates that you want to talk with someone. The more signals you can send that say "I'm approachable and, yes, I would like to talk with you too," the more others will feel comfortable conversing with you. Making eye contact is a really effective way of sending a message that you're approachable.

# 41

## Small, but Meaningful, Chat

A SUCCESSFUL CONVERSATION IS much like a tennis game—back and forth with each participant equally enthused. Once the dialogue has begun, the conversation should flow from there.

Mastering small talk will help you find common ground to create a mini-bond with new contacts. Small talk may feel trite and unimportant, but it's the small talk that leads to the big talk outside the event.

The goal of conversation at functions is to establish enough common ground to determine a reason to connect outside the event. Ideally small talk will uncover common interests, business alignments, the six degrees that separate you, potential need for your product or service, and basically whether or not you enjoy each other's company. The goal is not to become best friends or a new client on the spot. Although it's nice when those instant connections happen, usually that's not the case.

> **The goal of conversation at functions is to establish enough common ground to determine a reason to connect again.**

Keeping a conversation rolling is simple when you learn to listen and ask appropriate probing questions that naturally grow from the dialogue. You only need to prepare a couple of questions in advance. If there is a genuine connection then you can proactively engage in conversation.

When a person doesn't participate actively in a conversation with you, that's a red flag to say to yourself, "Okay, this is not one of my quality contacts, it's time to move on and meet someone else."

Ultimately, the decision each person has to make during this initial contact is whether or not there is enough connection to warrant future interaction. It's during these small conversations that people form their opinions about whether they like you, trust you, and believe you're competent.

Actual business talk is quite limited at functions. Learning what people do and perhaps about some of their big developments or projects is about the extent of the business talk expected. Deeper connections are formed through finding common ground that is not work related.

There is a balance between too much and too little business talk. If you don't talk business at all you may miss an opportunity to communicate who you are, what you do, and what you have to offer and that you are competent in your field. There are some people who you can know for years and never hear them talk about work. You just assume they are retired or not interested in more clients.

However, if you talk about your work too much you run the risk of boring others. Too much "shoptalk" can easily put a damper on an evening. Watch for cues from your conversation partners. How are they responding to the conversation with you? Are they engaged? Are they obviously looking for a new conversation partner? Are they listening to and understanding what you are saying? Are you giving them more information than they expect, want, or need? Are you monopolizing the conversation and not giving others a chance to share ideas or ask questions?

## Match the depth of dialogue to the environment.

Match the depth of dialogue to the environment. You don't want to let people overhear confidential or inappropriate information. Plus, talk that is too deep at business functions can lead to heated conversations. New contacts could be put on edge. Over-heated conversations can quickly be subdued by simply making a closing agreeable statement that offers little room for a rhetorical comment. This tactic will diffuse the situation quickly and without incident.

For example, say with a smile, "Well, that's one issue we're not going to solve tonight," or simply close the conversation with "I certainly understand your perspective," minus the "but" that is sitting on the tip of your tongue.

You won't win points for always having to be right. You may win the debate while making someone else look bad, but in the end, you'll make yourself look worse. You will, however, win points for having social graces if you are the bigger person and cool potentially fiery situations.

You have to know when to let go and kill the discussion even if you believe you are correct on the issue. In the grand scheme of things, we must value the opinions of others and accept that it is not important to win every debate. The last thing you want to do is to appear as the know-it-all who must end conversations as the perceived winner.

Debates definitely have a place in conversation and can be a great way to help you get to know people, but pick the time and place and be aware of the company around you. Intense debates can lead to arguments that rarely provide a comfortable environment at business and social functions, especially for those who aren't interested in the topic at hand.

Obviously, discussions around usually taboo subjects such as religion and politics will be discussed and debated at religious or political events. Even then, you want to be sure that the intensity level is kept to a professional standard. Earning a reputation as a hothead doesn't make it easy for people to like you, trust you, or believe you're competent.

Keep a close watch on people's body language. As the conversation intensifies, you may notice onlookers become tense. That's a good cue to cool it.

Another confrontational conversation style is playing "top it." Although at first everyone seems to be enjoying the banter, each turn becomes an exercise to see who can say something bigger, better, and more profound to outshine the other.

This habit can stem from a lack of self-confidence and a need to flex one's muscles to sound credible, but it backfires. "Top-it" conversationalists come across as arrogant and make the other person feel uncomfortable and unworthy. One-upmanship is a definite no-no.

Let others have the glory every now and again. A person may be sharing what he or she perceives to be an exciting story about a recent trip; let him or her tell it and bask in the moment. There's nothing worse than having someone pipe in to say, "Yeah, been there 10 times. No biggie. There are better places to go."

You'll squash the person's excitement and you'll purposely make another person feel inferior. No one cares that you've been to the destination 10 times if the information is offered with a condescending tone. However, input that is supportive and nonjudgmental is always welcome.

**Your words may be forgotten, but how you make people feel will be remembered.**

When it comes to small talk, don't think you must say something strikingly intelligent each time you speak. Your words may be forgotten, but how you make people feel will be remembered.

No doubt small talk can get a little dull after a while. So, take it upon yourself to make it interesting. To prepare for conversations, choose your five favorite safe topics. These will make it easy for you to swing an otherwise stale conversation into one that makes you a genuinely enthusiastic conversationalist.

Have you ever been in a conversation that just wasn't clicking, then suddenly the mood changes and you both have a smile on your face as the conversation starts firing on all cylinders? That's because you found common ground. It occurs when two people have an interest in the same topic.

By determining in advance what interests you, half of the equation for stimulating conversation is complete. Now your job is to guide the conversation from topic to topic until you solve the other important half of the equation: What's of interest to your new contact?

For example, one of my favorite topics is travel. Whenever conversation is directed to stories of where people have been, where they are going next, or where they would like to travel, I'm automatically enthused and interested.

**By determining in advance what interests you, half of the equation for stimulating conversation is complete.**

On the flip side, some topics make my eyes glaze over and my mind starts to wander. These uninteresting topics for me may be someone else's hot topics. The idea is to find the topics you both enjoy. If you find your conversation partner disengaging, then change the subject. Your arsenal of prepared conversation topics will give you ammunition when a conversation hits a lull and you need to give it some energy.

There are networking trainers who say that you should only worry about finding whatever interests your new contact and create the conversation from there. Sure, that's fine, but what about you? At what point does it become all about everyone else and not at all about who you are and what you want? It's important to find the balance. Those who pretend to care only about what interests others miss the chance to enjoy the process and to genuinely engage in a two-way relationship by sharing something about themselves and finding common bonds.

There are key pieces of information that will help you categorize your contacts and figure out where they fit in your life. (See Chapter 54: Categorizing Contacts.) You want to steer the conversation in a direction that reveals these relevant details to help you decide if this person is a qualified prospect in your target market without specifically asking them.

For example, if you own a wellness store, it would be helpful to direct the conversation to learn if the contact takes special care of his health, spends time exercising outdoors, or frequents the gym.

I must admit, after attending hundreds of events and interacting with thousands of people, there are times when I feel small talk is simply a dreaded requirement. I'm writing this so you know that I completely understand if you're reading this and thinking, "I don't care about all this superficial conversation."

When I get in those moods, I remind myself that the person I'm meeting has the potential to be my next big client or a newfound friend. If those thoughts don't shift my attitude, I'll set a personal challenge to create a super-duper fantastic conversation with a new contact. For some reason, this additional challenge seems to inspire me to get enthusiasm back into the small talk. If that doesn't work, I just remind myself that the person I'm talking with deserves my respect.

The real key to great conversations is to relax. Let the conversation flow naturally. That's easiest to do when you're fully engaged and genuinely interested in the conversation topic and the person with whom you are talking.

# 42

---

# Listening

YOUR MOST IMPORTANT RESPONSIBILITY during a conversation is to listen. For some people, it's also the most difficult part of the process. Listening requires focus, genuine interest, and a desire to want to hear and process what another person is saying. It also requires you to stop talking. Mastering listening skills will make creating dynamic conversations easier because you'll be able to pick up on small points, ask relevant questions, and take the dialogue in a new direction.

As you develop your conversational skills, make a conscious effort to become an excellent listener. The best advantage is that you will be a pleasant addition to any conversation. Good listeners are always welcomed—and needed. When you listen closely and purposely, you learn powerful information that is otherwise missed.

Most people like to hear themselves talk, so finding someone who will listen is quite refreshing. Pretending to listen won't separate you from your competition. Actually hearing and processing what a person has to say and then responding appropriately will.

**When you listen closely and purposely, you learn powerful information that is otherwise missed.**

A client once told me she was not a good listener. When I asked her why, she said she's usually not interested in what the other person is saying. It was a brutally honest and refreshing comment that reflects the reality of human nature. We only care about what we care about and we tend to shut out the rest.

Having your five favorite safe topics should help you maneuver a conversation to ensure the subject matter appeals to your interests. It's easier to listen when you want to hear the information being communicated. However, effective listening won't just happen by finding topics that interest you. The second important part of the solution is to have a genuine interest in the person who is doing the talking. Accomplishing this may require an attitude adjustment on your part. Perhaps focusing on your greater goal of building your ultimate network will motivate you to take a genuine interest in other people and what they are saying.

The sooner you can accept the importance of listening, the sooner you can perfect the skill and start connecting with your ultimate network.

Listening well takes patience. It means not saying everything your brain thinks it wants you to say. It's rude to interrupt people as they speak.

## Have a genuine interest in the person who is doing the talking.

Show you are listening by fully engaging with your conversation partner. Maintain eye contact (every seven or eight seconds glance away to avoid a hypnotic trance), nod your head, ask pertinent questions, and make statements that have relevance to the topic being discussed.

Be aware of your body language. What are you saying without speaking? By engaging your entire body in the listening process you'll become a better listener. It's tough for your ears to hear what the person in front of you is saying when your eyes are looking at someone else. Wandering eyes and a disengaged stance will give the impression that you are not interested. This is sending a negative message, rather than projecting a genuine, welcoming professional image that will encourage people to like you, trust you, and believe you are competent.

When you are fortunate to find a good listener, don't take advantage of the situation by doing all the talking. It's difficult for a person to listen for an extended length of time. Monopolizing the conversation to tell someone all about you restricts the back-and-forth dialogue required for the two of you to develop a mutually beneficial relationship. Keep an eye on your listener's body language and ask yourself, if you were that person, would you still be interested in listening to you?

# 43

## Creating Mini-Bonds

THE SECOND STEP IN THE Mingling Formula is essential to change casual contacts into business relationships. Learning how to create mini-bonds will make you a master at building genuine business relationships. Some networking trainers call this step "establishing rapport." To me, this sounds like an over-used phrase that conjures images of phony conversation and forced common interests.

Without a mini-bond, there is no reason to move to the third step, which is exchanging contact information. Rushing through the mini-bond step leads to mere business-card collecting and ineffective networking attempts.

A mini-bond means there was enough of a connection that you'll remember each other after the event and that the memory will be positive. A lot of what determines this level of connection is subconscious and relies on nonverbal cues. It's the few seconds where the person judges you to determine if you are of interest and vice versa. This is why spending time working on your personal brand in the Second Pillar is so important. It will help you maximize the impression you make. Granted, looking well-polished isn't enough to drive profitable networking, but it's the foundation upon which everything else rests.

The key to creating a mini-bond is actually caring about the other person. You can't fake this. It's tough to hide a genuine dislike for people and displaying a negative, uninterested attitude won't help people like you, trust you, or believe you are competent. If you truly don't like people, you may want to reconsider your decision to be in the people business. Overcoming a disinterest in others will require a shift in thinking. Do all you can to appreciate the talents and personalities of the people you meet. Finding the best in others while taking the focus off yourself is a good place to start.

What characteristics do people you connect with possess? What do you enjoy most about people? What is the difference between people you like and those you like less? Is it common interest, mutual friends, or similar humor?

Years ago a friend told me, "Love is not what you feel about another person; it's how another person makes you feel about yourself." I don't know if it's a famous quote or where it came from, but it has stuck with me.

## The more respect you show to others, the more respect you will earn for yourself.

As you build your network, you will notice that the better you make others feel about themselves, the more people will be attracted to you. Setting others at ease will make them feel comfortable and they will want to be around you. Conversely, if you are harsh, abrupt, and uninterested, it will have the opposite effect. The more respect you show to others, the more respect you will earn for yourself.

Body language can make a huge impact on your ability to establish rapport. Are your actions sending the right message? Do you seem engaged in the conversation? Are your eyes wandering to find someone more interesting? Are you "present" or are you worrying about your dry cleaning?

Make solid eye contact and square your body to your conversation partner. Focusing solely on the person will make him or her feel important. Surprisingly, 30 seconds of engaged dialogue has more impact than 10 minutes spent in disengaged, phony conversation.

Sharing a laugh or inside joke goes a long way to establishing a sense of ease and camaraderie.

Once you identify your favorite topics it will be easier to find connections with people. This will enable you to steer conversations in directions that interest you, thereby maximizing your chance to create a mini-bond based on common interest.

As you get to know contacts better, you will find the conversation with them will become more personal, more fluent, and more comfortable. This level of comfort is imperative to take casual contacts to the next level, provided you don't cross any inappropriate lines and personal boundaries.

There's a natural back and forth that goes with the release of information that allows a relationship to develop to a deeper connection. A block in the flow of information can cramp this process and leave relationships stagnant.

## There's a natural back and forth that goes with the release of information that allows a relationship to develop a deeper connection.

I'm not suggesting you need to divulge every secret about your life from infancy to adulthood. That's not appropriate behavior for professional relationships. However, until you engage in something more than the typical "How are you?" and "What do you do?" banter, you'll find it difficult to truly connect on a substantial level with others.

The intensity of a relationship is not determined by the quantity of information shared between two people, but rather, by the quality and depth of information that is shared. The more intimate the dialogue, the deeper the bond.

Think about what you're willing to share about yourself with a brand-new contact compared to what you tell your best friend. There is a big difference at the two ends of the spectrum and there is a variable scale for everyone in between.

A good friend commented that there was just something she didn't trust about a mutual associate. She said, "Something just isn't right." Her observation surprised me, but I was intrigued and open to hear her rationalization for this comment.

She asked if I'd noticed how this contact is totally private about her information, but always wants to know everything about everyone else. It feels like she's on the outside looking in, just collecting information rather than engaging in meaningful conversation.

My friend's perspective made sense. By never sharing her story, this individual did not make it easy for people to know, like, or trust her. She did not release any substance about herself, so she came across as having a hidden agenda, which did not endear her to people.

Looking back, I believe one of the reasons I developed such a vast network is because I am willing to share little parts of my life with people I like and with whom I feel I have a connection.

## The intensity of a relationship is not determined by the quantity of information that is shared, but by the quality and depth of information that is shared.

My life is an open book and, yes, to add another cliché, I wear my heart on my sleeve. Some would consider it a fault, but from my perspective, this kind of open attitude has made it easier for me to form deeper bonds with many people in a relatively short time.

As you increase the number of contacts you make, be prepared to open up so you can change those casual contacts into more important and meaningful relationships in your personal and professional life.

To become a master at creating mini-bonds keep asking yourself, "How am I making this other person feel?" Connections are as much about the emotional tie as the actual conversations. Sometimes people don't really consider how their actions affect the people around them. If you seem uninterested, the other person will return the favor. When you start to become more engaged, you'll notice others will follow suit and mini-bonds will be created naturally.

# 44

---

# Exchanging Contact Information

ONCE YOU'VE CREATED A MINI-BOND and decided you would like to connect with this person again, simply ask for a business card. (See Chapter 47: Business Cards.)

When you don't have an opportunity to get the card, simply remember who introduced you and ask that person to send you the contact details. You can also search the Internet for contact information. People who don't carry business cards may suggest you visit their website to touch base with them. If they ask you to contact them, be sure you do.

Don't rush to this step of the Mingling Formula. If a mini-bond was not created or there doesn't seem to be a reason to connect in the immediate future, it is not necessary to exchange contact coordinates. This would lead to mere business-card collecting.

You don't want to underestimate your ability to build rapport or you will never get people's contact information. You won't build your network if you don't take a chance by building relationships outside functions. Creating a mini-bond does not mean that you've become best friends. It's just that you've connected enough so the contact will remember you when you follow up or see him the next time.

If you don't exchange contact details, just take note of anything you discussed. The next time you run into each other mention a tidbit from your last conversation. Your memory of your first encounter will be an instant mini-bond generator.

Sometimes it takes months, or even years, before you actually want to connect with someone in a one-on-one setting. You may see a person every now and again, say hello, and ask how he or she is, but the relationship doesn't go any further than that. Those are your casual contacts and they will stay that way until you find a reason to take the relationship to the next level.

# 45

---

# Moving On

When I started my company, I had a breakfast meeting with a good friend who is a very successful businessman. I shared my plan for teaching people about business networking and everything the concept entailed.

He laughed and said, "What I need to know is how to end a conversation. The only thing I can think to say when I want to leave the discussion is 'I have to go to the bathroom.'" I chuckled as I thought, "I do see him in hallways going to and from the bathroom—a lot."

As it turns out, exiting a conversation gracefully is the trickiest part of the Mingling Formula, even more so than starting a conversation. People figure once they're in, they're in. To make events worthwhile, you need to talk with multiple people. Learning how to draw a conversation to a close is critical.

## The entire Mingling Formula should happen in 3 to 8 minutes.

For the most part, people don't want to end a conversation because they don't want to appear rude. Well, you're off the hook; the reverse is true. To monopolize someone's time is rude. The general rule of thumb is a maximum of 10 minutes for a conversation between two people at a business function or cocktail party. I'll give you even less. In my experience, the entire Mingling Formula should happen in 3 to 8 minutes.

Events are opportunities to meet new people and reconnect with current contacts. Thanks to your pre-event homework, you have specific people you hope to meet and others with whom you want to touch base. That can't happen if you spend all night talking with the same person, your best friends, or coworkers.

As an experiment, I once stayed in a corner with one person for an entire function. Naturally, people flowed by and we would engage in dialogue with others, but for several hours it was basically the two of us together. Thankfully, this person was incredibly engaging and we enjoyed our time together. I knew the majority of the people at the conference, so I wasn't concerned about mingling. Halfway through the night I thought, this guy must think no one else wants to talk with me or that I'm a snob and don't want to talk with them.

At the end of the evening, I was even more convinced of the importance of mingling through a room and moving from conversation to conversation. What happened that night was no different from what countless professionals do every time they walk into a room.

Spending all that time together in a loud room didn't mean that our relationship was now much deeper than if we had spent a portion of the time together. It would have made more sense to go to a restaurant to have an uninterrupted conversation, rather than stay among the crowd. The dialogue in a group setting is often less substantial than when you are speaking one-on-one.

Ending a conversation is often a relief for others. Do you really think the other person came to the event to spend his whole night talking with you? Most likely not! Once you get your head around the idea that it is okay to end a conversation, it will make it easier for you to do so without guilt.

There are three likely scenarios that can make it difficult to end a conversation:

1. Both parties would like to end the conversation, but neither knows how.
2. The conversation is really enjoyable and you don't want it to end.
3. Your conversation partner has identified you as a comfort zone and doesn't want you to leave because he or she will be left alone.

Fortunately, each type of conversation can be ended gracefully with the proper techniques. There are three ways to exit a conversation:

1. The verbal disengage
2. The third-party introduction
3. The "gotta-go" technique

## THE VERBAL DISENGAGE

It's easy to end conversations that fall into scenarios 1 and 2. Know that it's better to end the conversation on a high note and leave lots to talk about when you reconnect outside the event. If you hang on too long, you may overstay your welcome. This is a perfect situation for a verbal disengage. Simply have your closing lines ready to end the conversation politely. Some examples of conversation closers are:

- "I'd like to chat with you more about this. Why don't we grab a coffee sometime outside this busy event?" By offering a comment that suggests you'll meet again somewhere else at another time, the contact will not be offended at all and you've already established a reason to connect later.
- "Do you have a business card?" is the perfect way to say, "I'm interested in communicating with you further, but our time together at this event has come to an end."
- "That's great. It was Bill, right?" Offer a short closing comment that offers validation to the conversation ("That's impressive" or "No doubt you should be pleased with those results") and then re-establish his name. This is helpful if you didn't catch his name at the beginning.
- "Well, Joe, it's been great talking with you. I'm glad I ran into you" is a natural closing line that prompts an almost immediate close.

### Verbal disengage: change the tone of the conversation to indicate it has come to an end.

I find this last exit line extremely effective even outside business functions when you just casually run into people, or when you want to close a meeting. The whole idea is to change the tone of the conversation to indicate it is time to part ways.

**The Verbal Disengage Formula:**
Transition Word + Name + Relevant Statement (+ Next Step)

The last example above fits this formula very well: "Well (*transition word*), Joe (*name*), it's been great running into you (*relevant statement*), we should grab a coffee in the next few weeks (+ *next step*)." Closing with a next step is optional. It's only required if there is in fact a next step.

Use transition words, such as *well*, *gosh*, or *you know*, to change the direction of the conversation. These words act like verbal commas.

The name is just a nice closer. Most people use names at the beginning and end of conversations, not in the middle of it, so it's a subtle cue that the conversation is ending.

A complementary relevant statement gives the conversation closure. It recaps what you've done (run into each other, had a great conversation). Ideally, put it into the past tense to offer another subtle cue that indicates the end of the conversation.

Potentially add a next-step question or comment such as "Do you have a business card?" or "We should go for lunch/play golf/go for coffee" or "Call me when those tickets go on sale." *Only* suggest a next step if you genuinely plan on following through on the suggestion. Otherwise you risk ruining your credibility by leaving a trail of false promises hanging in the universe.

This disengagement technique is easy to implement anywhere.

A fellow board member and I were having a meeting in the lounge of our dining club. A gentleman who was upstairs attending a private function wandered downstairs and sat in a big comfy lounge chair beside us to join our conversation.

He was a very pleasant man and although we certainly enjoyed the conversation with him, this board member and I had a tight time frame and pressing issues to discuss. There was no time for any more idle chitchat.

So I simply offered a "Well, so-and-so, am I ever glad you wandered downstairs to say hello. It's been great meeting you." The gentleman returned the sentiment, stood up, shook our hands, and with a smile on his face went back upstairs. It took all of 30 seconds to politely disengage him from our conversation. It's difficult to know how long the conversation would have continued without my closing statement. Also, I suspect he was equally relieved to have the green light to return to his function.

## THE THIRD-PARTY INTRODUCTION

The second exit strategy, called the third-party introduction, is another great option to close a conversation gracefully. It's especially effective with scenario 3, when you are speaking with someone who simply doesn't want you to leave. This exit strategy capitalizes on the natural dance that happens as people mingle around a room.

To take advantage of this gracious exit, you simply introduce your contact to another person and once they start their own conversation, you allow them to chat while you begin a conversation with someone new.

Third-party introductions work best if you are in a high-traffic area. It's tough to have someone casually walk by and join the conversation if you're stuck in, or near, a corner. However, if no one happens to be conveniently nearby, you could suggest that both of you go over to so-and-so because you would like to introduce her to him.

When scenario 3 happens, the third-party introduction is your best bet because people who are shy or introverted may be concerned that if you leave them, they won't find anyone else to talk with and will be left standing alone.

Don't leave someone hanging, but at the same time, you have to respect yourself and not allow others to monopolize your time. Be kind, but understand that others are not your responsibility.

### Respect yourself and don't allow others to monopolize your time.

When you just can't shake someone, it's helpful to know that it's virtually impossible to go to an auction table with a person and leave the area with that same person. Inevitably you'll get separated.

## THE "GOTTA-GO" TECHNIQUE

As a last resort, you can use the "gotta-go" technique. Chances are you've used this exit strategy before. "I've gotta-go to the auction table, bar, restroom . . ."

To save your credibility when using this technique, if you say you've "gotta go," then that means you've got to go where you said you were going. It's rather insulting to be left by someone who is supposedly going to the bathroom, only to see that person walk directly to the bar to fill up with more liquid. That type of white lie chips away at your credibility. Use the "gotta-go" strategy sparingly.

# 46

# Breaking into Group Discussions

ASIDE FROM HOW TO exit conversations, the other question I am asked most frequently is how to break into group discussions. Groups can lead to great conversations and new introductions, so it's a worthwhile skill to learn.

The trick to breaking into group discussions is to first notice the dynamics of the group. What is the intensity level? Are two people having a personal conversation? If so, that's not the time to interrupt. Their focus will be on their own issues rather than on getting to know you.

However, if you notice two people together who look disengaged or bored, that's the perfect time to wander over and infuse some energy into their conversation. You'll be more than welcome.

It is rude to interrupt two people who are talking and then engage only one of them in dialogue, ignoring the other. When this happens to you, have the social grace to bridge back to the original conversation partner rather than leaving him or her standing on the outside of the circle.

Look for larger groups having fun. The tone for people to be included is already set. Make eye contact with someone in the group. Most likely he will see your intention to join and open a space for you.

If you are familiar with a group participant, a gentle hand on the person's upper back can let him know you are there and wanting to join. Once a member of the group acknowledges your presence and you have a feel for the group dynamics, offer input into the group discussion.

**Notice the dynamics of the group before breaking into the conversation.**

When you are already part of a group, act as a host or hostess. Always open the circle to others trying to enter. One day they will return the favor. If one person monopolizes the conversation, feel free to ease the transition to another person by shifting the focus from the talker and asking for input from another. "That's quite interesting, Bill. Scott, what do you think?" This will encourage others to participate and feel like part of the group.

When a person enters your group discussion, it's best to finish your sentence or allow the person speaking to do so and then acknowledge the newcomer. If you are mid-story, once you've acknowledged the new person, resume the conversation already in progress, with the new person included. Once that thought is complete, then you can officially welcome the newcomer to the group. You might say something such as "Bob's just telling us about his recent vacation." Then return to the conversation and allow Bob to continue to lead the dialogue.

If the story was complete, you can bridge the conversation by saying something like "Bob's just told us about his recent vacation. What about you, have you had any travel adventures lately?" This will give the newcomer an opportunity to contribute to the conversation.

As a newcomer to a group, be patient and allow the person speaking to finish his or her sentence. It's awkward when you know someone is waiting in the wings, but then because the conversation didn't come to a grinding halt, he or she turned and walked away, probably assuming that you weren't interested in talking. A little patience goes a long way in this instance because sooner or later there will be an opening in the conversation.

Group dynamics are constantly shifting. Two or more conversations will naturally spin off from the original group and smaller groups will form. The sheer nature of the progression of group conversations should eliminate any intimidation entering a group conversation may present to you.

# 47

# Business Cards

BUSINESS CARDS ARE THE single most cost-effective marketing tool you can use. It's not about collecting and handing out mass quantities of business cards. The actual cards are just pieces of paper. The real value is the people who are represented by the information on the cards.

Carrying business cards is a no-brainer. Without a business card, how will contacts know how to reach you? It's your calling card for your professional life. Even though they can be ordered in large quantities, it's not quantity that leads to a profitable network, so use cards wisely.

Among negative networking connotations is the image of a salesman walking into a function and handing out his card randomly to absolutely everyone who walks through the door. What are the chances those people will call him? Slim to none. In North America, the appropriate exchange of business cards is between two people who have met, had a conversation, and created a mini-bond.

**The appropriate exchange of business cards is between two people who have met, had a conversation, and created a mini-bond.**

There are some who defend the position that they won't give out cards; they will only take cards so they can control the follow-ups and avoid hearing from people they don't like. This seems shortsighted to me. If you receive and give a card you still have the same control. Sure, every now and again you will give your card to a person who will follow up repeatedly and add you to mailing lists without your permission. Just unsubscribe. That's a risk of doing business and that's why you have technology with spam controls.

Imagine the possibilities if you share your card even when you don't feel like it.

What if Joe meets Bill at a conference and after a brief conversation decides not to give out his coveted business card. Joe doesn't "control" the follow-up as he intended to because he gets busy or doesn't see the point in contacting Bill.

Later that week, Bill is enjoying dinner with his wife, Sarah, who happens to be the human resources manager for one of Joe's target companies. Sarah casually mentions she's pulling together the list of speakers for the company's upcoming sales conference.

Bill says, "Oh, I met a speaker at the conference. The guy who introduced us said he was a really good speaker and he seemed like a nice guy." Sarah responds, "Great, I'll check him out. Do you have his contact details?" Bill says, "No, actually I don't. He didn't give me his business card. I gave him my card, but I haven't heard from him since." Sarah says, "Oh, too bad." End of story.

Like so many other professionals who don't carry or hand out business cards, Joe thinks that possibility would never happen. How would Joe know? He's too busy trying to grow his business staring at a box of his own business cards.

It's amazing what happens when you make it easy for people to know who you are, what you do, and what you have to offer. Crazier stories than the one above have resulted from business-card exchanges. That's the beauty of networking. You never know where contacts can lead. Bill's wife has to hire a speaker; we don't know if Joe would have been hired for the job, but at the very least, he would have been considered.

Bottom line: don't prejudge and don't hoard your business cards. Professionals must carry and give business cards. Period.

It is your responsibility to give yourself a chance for success. Not giving business cards either because you forgot them or you want to keep control of your contacts makes it difficult for people to know how to reach you.

## Have an "inbox" and an "outbox" for your business cards.

At functions, anticipate that people will ask you for your business card. Be prepared. To avoid the unprofessional search or accidental grab of another's card, establish an "inbox" and an "outbox" for your business cards.

Men, you have it easy—one pocket in, one pocket out. Ladies, it's helpful to buy purses with pockets on the outside so cards are easily accessible with one hand without you having to open your purse. When cards are inside the purse, be sure to organize and minimize the contents of your handbag before the function so contacts don't see a mess or unmentionables inside your purse.

As stylish as cardholders may look, they are not user-friendly devices at functions. They require two hands to operate—one to open and hold the case and one to remove the card. You have to put down your drink or fumble with your purse while your newest contact watches you go through the awkward exercise with your cardholder. It just adds an unnecessary step that, if eliminated, would add another touch of polish to your image.

In North America, the exchange of business cards happens as an afterthought. In some cultures, the exchange of business cards is a ritual that demands respect. I'd be happy if we could at least meet in the middle.

## When you receive a card, read it in front of the person rather than just throwing it into your pocket or purse.

For starters, slow down the exchange. When you receive a card, actually look at it right away, while you're in front of the person who gave it to you. Read it, notice it, and look at the person again. Who have you just met? Reading the card will help you create a mental snapshot of the person and his name together. Recall the earlier section about remembering names. Business cards, when used properly, can be a huge help in this regard.

The information you just read on the card may spark a question or comment that can lead to a deeper conversation or mutual point of reference. Thank the person for his card and put it into your "inbox."

After the event, empty the cards from your inbox. Write all the details you can remember about each person on the back of the card. When and where did you meet? Who introduced you? What did you discuss? Are there follow-up actions required? Once you have categorized the contact (See Chapter 54: Categorizing Contacts), you can set the cards aside in your "to enter" box on your desk.

A trick a good friend of mine uses to remember whether further action is required is to dog-ear the card or he presses his fingernail into the card to mark it before he puts it into his pocket. When he reviews his cards after the function, the ones with the folds or indentations go to the priority follow-up pile.

Once a week, enter all the new business-card contacts into your electronic management system. Include all contact details and all of your notes.

Your reference notes will come in handy in the future when your contact calls. You can have a quick peek and remind yourself where and when you met, what you talked about, and who connected you. You will impress the person simply because you cared enough to remember things about him from your initial meeting. This will go a long way to making you likeable.

The beauty of using your business cards in this manner is that it makes you think about your new contact six times:

1. when you were introduced;
2. when you accepted the business card;
3. when you wrote details on the card;
4. when you categorized the contact;
5. when you entered the information; and
6. when you filed the business card.

Thinking about contacts after you meet them will help you remember their names and details about them. So often we meet people but never think about them again. Each time you think about a new contact, you solidify your mental snapshot of that person.

### Each time you think about a new contact, you solidify your mental snapshot of that person.

The process may seem like tedious work, but it takes mere minutes. The benefits gained from these efforts will be long-lasting. How do you put a price tag on remembering people? What if remembering that person meant you were able to connect the next time you saw him and he became your client?

Finding a business-card system that works for you is imperative to building a profitable network. The cost of not having a proper system and running the risk of forgetting those you've met is far too great. If you care about building your network, you have to treat your efforts to connect with people seriously. That means tracking and managing your contacts effectively, regardless of how daunting a task it seems.

# 48

# Communicating YOU

## *The 5-10-15-Second Communication*

THE TWO MOST PREDICTABLE QUESTIONS that will be asked when you meet someone are "Do you have a business card?" and "What do you do?"

Unfortunately, these are the two questions that are the most difficult for many professionals to answer appropriately and with confidence. After the last section, I'm hopeful that you'll never be caught without a business card again. Now we need to solve the seemingly mysterious second question.

A good friend once said, "If a person can't clearly tell me what he does between nine and five every day, how can he expect me to use his services and trust that he knows what he's doing?" It's a good point. Somewhere along the line the answer to this simple question became complicated.

Remember, it's your responsibility to make it easy for people to know who you are, what you do, and what you have to offer. So when you're asked what you do, establish enough understanding about your deliverables so your contact understands what you do. This is your first opportunity to educate your new contact about what you do and what you have to offer.

Earlier in the book we established that networking is an exercise in education and connection, not sales. That means you do not need to go into a huge sales pitch when asked this question at business functions.

The goal is to establish enough understanding so that when your contacts need your product or service, or know someone who does, they will think to call or recommend you first. You want to plant the seed for future, more in-depth business discussions outside the mingling environment.

## People don't need to know every little idiosyncrasy about your company.

People need to understand the basics of what you do and what you have to offer, but they don't need to know every little idiosyncrasy about your company to make the decision to use your services, buy your product, or recommend you to someone who will. Once they know the basics, the rest of the decision to do business with you is primarily influenced emotionally, based on whether they like you, trust you, and think you're competent. There will be opportunities to communicate more significant information outside the function, once a potential fit for your services is identified.

You may have heard of the 30-second elevator pitch. It's a popular concept that has you sum up your company in a 30-second commercial. The motivation behind it was that if you found yourself in an elevator face-to-face with a potential investor, you could communicate a summary of your entire business before the elevator ride was finished.

When was the last time you had to promote your company during a short ride in an elevator?

A 30-second elevator pitch is perfect when you need to stand in front of an audience and give a fast blurb about your company. It is also effective when you need to give a synopsis of your company in a more formalized setting such as a sales meeting, introductory phone call, or a one-on-one encounter outside a mingling environment.

A solid explanation of your business and your value proposition are expected and appropriate in those situations. In fact, most networking associations dedicate a portion of their formal program for members to share information about their businesses.

## The concept of the 30-second elevator pitch does not transition well into real conversations at business functions.

Unfortunately, the concept of a 30-second elevator pitch does not transition well into real conversations at business functions. Most professionals feel they have to compact their entire business into an infomercial. Infomercials exist to sell you something and since networking is not selling, the two concepts don't work together.

Your focus is building relationships, finding needs, and, when there's a fit, moving into the sales process later, outside the function. Sales will naturally come from educating people on who you are, what you do, and what you have to offer, from connecting with them positively and showing them you are competent.

While you're mingling, remember that people will connect with who you are first and what you do second.

A professional who takes this 30-second, canned approach to telling someone what he or she does will lose the conversation partner's interest after about 5 seconds of rhetoric. His or her mind will likely drift to something that's more important. After experiencing a plethora of uncomfortable and ineffective answers to this question, I decided there must be a better way for professionals to communicate what they do using a natural conversational approach. Therefore, I developed what I like to call the 5-10-15-Second Communication.

My 5-10-15-Second Communication strategy will keep you from sounding like an infomercial. You still communicate the important details about what you do and what you have to offer, but you do it in a way that is conversational, inviting, and natural. It also allows the person who asked the question to be involved in the conversation and saves you from making a pitch to someone who isn't remotely interested in hearing one.

The 5-10-15-Second Communication adapts according to the conversation. Here's how it works:

Question: What do you do?
Answer: Your 5-second spot presents your core deliverable.

Allow your new contact to ask a question or comment on your statement.

Response: Your 10-second spot tells them what they need to know so they can understand what you do and a bit about what you have to offer.

Again, allow a question or comment from the person.

Response: Your 15-second spot tells them what they want to know.

If the new contact doesn't make an acknowledging comment or ask a relevant question after you've responded to his opening question with your 5-second spot, then there is no reason to continue to the next step.

To illustrate, here's an example of my 5-10-15-Second Communication:

Question: What do you do?
My under-5-second sound bite: "I teach profitable networking."

That simple comment will usually prompt a response, either in the form of a comment or a question. This statement will give me the cue to elaborate. If they do not respond in any way that invites further comment from me, I will assume they are not genuinely interested in more information. I realize that sometimes people just ask this question because they don't know what else to ask.

In that case, they aren't truly interested in the answer to their question. By not responding in a way that invites further comment, they have self-identified as "not interested" in more information. I don't take a lack of response as a personal insult. Not everyone is expected to be interested in my line of work or to need my services.

It's better to save my breath and avoid the sales-pitch experience. If a person is not interested in more than 5 seconds of what you have to say, imagine how uncomfortable it would be if you gave them a full 30-second explanation of unsolicited information.

Most times you can expect the conversation to go to the 10-second stage. You can usually predict what response will come after the 5-second blurb. In my experience, it's not much. It's often a simple "Oh really?" but it's enough to prompt me to go to the next stage of the dialogue.

My 10-second response communicates what I believe they need to know. It could sound something like this: "Yes, I wrote a book on personal branding and networking. Companies hire me to train their teams and speak at conferences so they can get better results." This response changes depending on the flow of conversation, but it's 10 seconds or less of information. Within those 10 seconds, there are two key facts I will share:

1. I'm a speaker for hire.
2. I help people become more effective at networking and have some general easy-to-identify credibility doing this because I wrote a book.

This approach is about education versus sales. By this point I've given them enough information that they understand fairly clearly what I do (I teach people profitable networking) and what I have to offer (I will help them be more profitable when they network).

Do you notice how I don't give them the title of my book, my company name, my website, or any other specifics that will be lost in mingling conversation? If they ask, then great, but the focus is on the value you deliver.

Their response after my 10-second spot will determine the future direction of the conversation. They may simply say, "Cool," which does not solicit any further information. That's fine; my job is complete. I will simply change the subject. If the person chooses to come back to the topic of my business later, we'll talk about it in a more in-depth manner.

On the other hand, if their response after my 10-second spot indicates a desire for more information, I move into my 15-second spot.

## It's about finding their interest in your deliverables and building a conversation around it.

The 15-second spot can go in countless directions, depending on the question asked or the comment that was given by the new contact. The 5-10-15-Second Communication allows the flexibility to go with the flow of an effective conversation. The 15-second spot is less about what I want to communicate and more about what they've asked to know. It's about finding their interest in my deliverables and building a conversation around it.

This is the key to turning the standard question "What do you do?" into a relevant (to the other person) conversation. It is so much more effective than spewing a 30-second sales pitch that may or may not be of interest.

**Example 1**
Comment: I hear the speakers' industry has a lot of potential.
My 15-second response would talk about the industry and my aspirations for being a part of it. I would allow them to lead the conversation as it interests them. It's about finding common ground in the speakers' industry.

**Example 2**
Comment: We hire speakers for my company all the time.
This is the best-case scenario because the contact has self-identified as a potential client. After the business function, I would move into the sales process with the contact, but for now we're still in networking mode, which involves education and connection. My response in a situation like this would simply be "Oh, that's great. Maybe there would be a fit for my sessions at your

company. I would be happy to send you some details and we can go from there." This is a perfect time to get his business card and end the business talk unless he keeps it going.

If I were to go into a full sales pitch at this point, I would run the risk of over-selling and annoying the person, making him or her regret mentioning that his or her company hires speakers. The person did not attend the function to close a deal with me. I recognize and respect that. The real business discussion is saved for outside the function.

Once I'm satisfied there is a potential fit for my services, I'll establish that I'll follow up in the near future. At this point, strengthening the personal connection becomes the priority. The goal is to be sure that the contact remembers me and wants to pick up the phone when I call. It's during the follow-up meeting and through forwarded information that I can communicate the true value I can offer his or her company.

# 49

---

# Developing Your Own 5-10-15-Second Communication

To RECAP:

- Your 5-second spot is your core deliverable.
- Your 10-second spot tells them what they need to know.
- Your 15-second spot tells them what they want to know.

## STEP 1: YOUR 5-SECOND SPOT

*Determine your core deliverable. In a nutshell, what do you do?*
What do you do? It's easy to want to sugarcoat this answer to create some poetic response to what should be a simple answer. What you do may sound boring, but it's what you do. What makes you appealing is your personality, your value, and how you present yourself, not phrases that make your work sound more exciting than it is.

Lines such as "It's tough to explain" or "I help people make their dreams come true" or "I help people find the light in the darkness" are too abstract and difficult to understand at functions and make it difficult for others to take you seriously. Put yourself in the other person's shoes. What are comments like that supposed to mean? Are you a top-secret agent? Do you work for Disney? Are you an electrician?

Depending on your personality and what your job is, you may be able to get away with an abstract summary about what you do, but for most of us, it's best to be up front and honest. Whatever your profession, you'll appear more successful if you are clear and confident as you communicate what you do. Hiding behind fluffy phrases will project a sense that you're withholding something, ashamed of what you do, or unprofessional. As an investment advisor, you need to educate contacts that you're an investment advisor. Not clearly communicating this fact will make it difficult for people who need an investment advisor to choose you or refer you to others who do. The same applies regardless of your profession.

A client expressed concern that people want to run away from him when they find out he sells insurance. Many people have told me they feel the same way about their professions. In my client's case, the reality is, at some point, the people he's interacting with will need insurance. Since he specializes in a specific field, it is likely they could purchase insurance from him. Not letting people know he sells insurance and his area of expertise will keep them from becoming his client because they won't understand what he does and what he has to offer.

His fear can be overcome by presenting a genuine, welcoming, professional image that encourages people to interact with him on a personal level. Not trying to sell them insurance on the spot, but rather focusing on making authentic connections, will dispel any potentially negative image associated with a certain industry or profession.

## STEP 2: YOUR 10-SECOND SPOT

*What are the two most important things people need to know about what you do?*
What does someone need to know about you to decide to buy your product or use your services? What seeds need to be planted to give a reasonable perspective of your professional value? Again, your 10-second communication shouldn't be complicated. It needs to be clear and easy to understand. When formulating your response, brainstorm ideas that need to be communicated. Then formulate them into point-form notes. Know the general gist of what you need to say and then let the sentences form naturally when you're in a conversation. This approach is more effective than blurting out a canned speech. It is vitally important to make your 10-second spot as simple as possible.

In my example above, I've given enough information and planted a seed so that when my contact needs to hire a speaker or is complaining about networking not being effective, it will trigger the thought, "I think that's what Allison teaches; maybe she can help us."

## STEP 3: YOUR 15-SECOND SPOT

*What are the likely questions new contacts may ask you about your work and how could you turn those answers into deeper conversations?*
This is your opportunity to prove you are competent. Listen to the comments or questions and answer them openly and honestly. Be flexible with the direction in which the person wants to take the conversation. Limit yourself to 15-second answers. Don't go on endlessly or the person will regret asking you to expand on the topic.

If you know your stuff (and you should because you live it daily), addressing these comments and questions should be easy. As soon as you've identified that a person is interested in your product or service, acknowledge intentions to follow up. Resist the urge to go into sales mode. Focus on building the relationship. If you haven't already done so, now is a good time to switch the emphasis from you to your contact. Get him or her talking and sharing.

Again, perspective, preparation, and practice are paramount to delivering a solid 5-10-15-Second Communication and successfully educating others about who you are, what you do, and what you have to offer.

- **Perspective:** When someone asks you what you do, they are not looking for a long-winded, in-depth answer. They just need to know enough to decide if they want to know more. Your connection could come from a topic that is not work related, so getting too hung up on being sure contacts know everything about your work could stifle your ability to find common ground in other areas that are more interesting to them.

  Allow time for the relationship to build. Eventually they may need your services or know someone who does and that's when they'll get all the "goods" about what you have to offer.

- **Preparation:** When you know the key messages you need to communicate, you will be able to formulate naturally flowing conversations around these bullet points.

- **Practice:** The more you communicate who you are, what you do, and what you have to offer, using my 5-10-15-Second Communication strategy, the easier and more effective you will become at communicating YOU.

# 50

# General Business Etiquette

## GRAMMAR AND SPELLING

"C U L8R" IS NOT A SENTENCE; "See you later" is. Texting has become the norm. These short forms, used by the masses, myself included, are replacing acceptable written and verbal communication skills. As a young professional who wants to connect with more-established professionals, leave these short forms for your best friends and others who speak in text talk.

Starting a conversation with "Yo! Wassup?" creates a completely different gut feeling about a person than "Hello! How are you?" To be taken seriously as a professional, using the second phrase would be more impressive than the first.

Addressing people as "girl," "hon," "sweetie," "babe," "dude," "bro," etc. is inappropriate in business settings. Make sure all of your professional interactions are just that—professional. While these nicknames can seem like they create a tighter bond and familiarity, they can make others feel uncomfortable. It's just not worth the risk.

Don't underestimate the power of following grammar rules as you build your personal brand. When you communicate with others in the business realm through writing, use a dictionary and style guide to check your spelling, punctuation, and grammar in e-mail and handwritten correspondence. Spell- and grammar-check software features are good in a pinch, but they are prone to context errors. One of my pet peeves is using the word "that" to reference a "who." A good (and concise) resource is *The Elements of Style* by William Strunk and E.B. White.

## E-MAIL

The easier you make it for people to get in touch with you, the more likely they will. A great way to do that is to make your contact details highly visible on all your communication.

A full electronic "signature" including your name, company name, mailing address, phone number(s), website, and e-mail address should be on the bottom of every e-mail you send, including replies and e-mails sent from your mobile device. It's a simple courtesy that can make it easy for people to add you to their electronic address books, find your number when it's better to answer via the telephone, or locate your office address when they are running late for a meeting.

Signatures only take you a few minutes to create, but will save your contacts time because they won't have to hunt for ways to reach you. Not everyone inputs data into an address book routinely so if you don't send your contact details, they may not have them handy. I've actually given up trying to respond to people when it becomes too time-consuming to track down their contact information.

Another great line to add to your mobile device signature is to reference that you are sending this note from a mobile device. Currently, my mobile signature states: "As this e-mail has been sent from my mobile device, please forgive any spelling mistakes, grammatical errors, word short forms and brief responses. My thumbs are fast typers, but not always accurate. ☺" You'd be surprised how many people comment positively on this disclaimer.

The idea originally came from an accountant who is fairly abrupt as a norm, but even more so on his mobile. He simply stated, "Please forgive short responses; this is sent from my BlackBerry." Easy enough, and it protects your professionalism if you do make a mistake.

Forwarding jokes and chain e-mails should be saved for friends, not for business associates. In fact, at this point in e-mail evolution, your friends would likely appreciate it if you stopped forwarding them too. Having time to forward these notes sends a message that you're not very busy at work. If an e-mail is particularly funny or has a certain relevance to a particular contact, send him a targeted forward, not an e-mail to your entire distribution list.

**Whenever you send something via
e-mail it is permanently out there.**

Emotions are very difficult to communicate via e-mail. If an issue requires sensitivity, pick up the phone instead. Keep in mind that whenever you send something via e-mail, it is permanently out there in cyberspace. It can be forwarded to anyone or read by the wrong person. It only takes one negative incident to make a person leery of e-mail security. For those of us who communicate best by the written word, this requires some learned discipline.

Keep an eye on your spam folder. Many a message has been lost thanks to overzealous spam filters. If you don't hear back from a contact, and the e-mail required a response, then wait an appropriate amount of time to make a follow-up call.

Before following up on nonurgent e-mails, allow three to seven days, including a weekend, as a courtesy for people to catch up on their messages. The person could be swamped or perhaps your message was filtered through spam and wasn't delivered. When you call to inquire about the missing response, don't put the contact on the defensive by accusing him of ignoring your e-mail or even subtly suggesting this has happened.

Simply say, "I wanted to follow up by telephone just in case you didn't receive my initial e-mail." He will likely apologize and mention his hectic schedule. Respond by empathizing and, hopefully, you will get the required details at that time.

The expectation nowadays is that people will respond instantly to your e-mail. While that is sometimes the case, for certain items, it may require more consideration than a quick on-the-spot response. Just because they see your message doesn't mean they are going to drop everything to respond to it right away. People who receive hundreds of e-mails a week (some receive hundreds in a day) need a break too.

BlackBerrys, iPhones, and Androids, whichever your preference, have made downtime a reality of the past. Even when we're on vacation, most of us are still monitoring incoming mail; some are easier to respond to immediately, some replies make more sense to wait till you are back in the office.

## When you are on vacation, use an out-of-office notification. If you receive one from someone, respect it.

When you are on vacation, use an out-of-office notification. If you receive one from someone, respect it.

Over the Christmas and New Year's break, I had more than one person e-mail me twice and call me twice to talk to me about different products.

I answered one call because I was curious about the urgency of the situation with a repeat number showing up on my call display. I asked her if she had received my out-of-office message and she confirmed that indeed she had! I was thinking, then why are you calling me again to talk about business when my out-of-office clearly stated I was unavailable until the New Year?

One friend says she ignores out-of-office notifications and expects people to respond anyhow because they usually do. Sure, that's true, but you can't assume they will answer all your e-mails and it's disrespectful to continually follow up before they are back from their indicated time away. As a business traveler, I'm guilty of monitoring my e-mails when I have the out-of-office notification activated. If I'm waiting for an airplane or before leaving the hotel room, I'll catch up on e-mails, but I'm still "away" and once I get to my destination, I'll be completely focused on my client, not my e-mails.

Use the blind carbon copy (BCC) function whenever you send group e-mails, unless you are expecting people to "Reply All." This cuts down on unnecessary e-mails when you're trying to arrange times for meetings or sending details about an event. Plus, it's inconsiderate to send someone's e-mail address to an entire group. Although they shouldn't, anyone who has a blast e-mail distribution list could copy those addresses for their own use.

## TELEPHONE COMMUNICATION

Technology has eliminated a lot of telephone communication. Often you'll find yourself leaving a voice mail rather than connecting with a live person.

From a time-management perspective, it takes longer to listen to voice messages and return calls than it does to answer a phone call on the first ring. Set a standard to return voice messages within a set time frame. Responding within 24 hours or by the end of the business day are good rules to adopt. Doing this shows respect for others.

When you leave a voice message, be sure to state your name and telephone number slowly and clearly. Leave your name and number once at the outset of the message and again at the close of the message. That way, the listener has a second chance to write your number and he or she can hear it twice without listening to the entire message again.

Tell the person why you're calling so he or she can prepare for the return call, understands the urgency of the situation, and can estimate the approximate time required for the return call.

Depending on the nature of the message you leave, it may be a different person who returns your call. Executives will often have their assistant call to arrange a meeting. The assistant will only call you if the executive has agreed to meet with you, so don't be offended; it's just effective time management.

## Messages that play hard to get or leave a mystery as to why you're calling lack professionalism.

Messages that play hard to get or leave a mystery as to why you're calling lack professionalism. When you're networking well, the person on the receiving end will be happy to take your call, even if it's to say he or she can't help you.

I'm a big fan of voice messages that say you'll send an e-mail in case that's an easier option for them to respond to you. That way, you've taken the extra step to make the phone call, but still you've offered the ease of responding through e-mail.

A typical voice message from me to a prospective client would be: "Hi, so-and-so, this is Allison Graham calling: 1-877-479-1462. As we discussed at last week's event, I'm just touching base to discuss a potential fit for my services with your company. I will send you an e-mail with some available dates in case that's an easier way for us to connect. Again, it's Allison Graham, 1-877-479-1462. I look forward to hearing from you either by e-mail or telephone."

The follow-up e-mail reads: "As promised in my voice message, I am sending you some available dates to meet to discuss a potential fit for my services. (Insert dates here) are still open. Hopefully one of these dates will work for you. If not, please let me know some alternative dates so we can go from there. Thanks!"

Phrases such as "just following up" and "as promised" subtly communicate that you are trustworthy and follow through on your commitments. Delivering the little things will slowly but surely earn you a reputation as someone who is credible and competent.

Limit the use of the word "I" in your written communication. Most of my sentences are structured to avoid introducing a thought with "I"; especially when you want someone to respond, it needs to be all about them, not about you. Take the above example. Most would write it as "I am hopeful that one of these dates will work", but instead, it's changed to, "Hopefully one of these dates will work for you." It's subtle, but an effective way to use e-mail.

If it's a quick fact that needs to be communicated, such as "The dress code for tomorrow's dinner is black tie," then simply leave this information on the voice message. Leaving a message that says "Give me a call and I'll let you know about the dress code for tomorrow night" generates more back-and-forth activity than busy people can handle. If you can, close the loop on the call and avoid telephone tag. In that case, I would send an e-mail or text with the details.

The key to using the phone effectively is to respect the other person. Long phone conversations should be reserved for family and friends, not business associates unless you've scheduled what I call a Virtual Coffee Meeting. This is when you schedule a phone call with the anticipation of get-to-know-you chitchat rather than just a quick, specific-issue phone call that is usually appropriate for business. It's great for when your schedule is too busy to meet in person or when you travel a lot for work. Scheduling a time for a phone call gives you a chance to talk.

When you do connect live with a person over the phone, be aware of his or her tone. You can tell when the person on the other end of the line is in a rush. Forcing the person to exchange pleasantries could be annoying when he or she just needs to hear the bare facts from you.

Hearing a stark "Hello" on the other end of the telephone line usually means the conversation should get to the point. Asking about the family and how everyone is enjoying the weather will likely frustrate your listener in these cases more than it will establish rapport.

You have no way of knowing what a person is doing when you call on the phone. He could be walking into a meeting, handling a crisis, or sitting at his desk playing solitaire out of boredom. Listen for clues and mirror your contact's pace as best you can.

**It's better to deal with the business up front and naturally broach the personal questions to find common ground as the call progresses.**

It's better to deal with the business up front and naturally broach the personal questions to find common ground as the call progresses. When you engage in extended pleasantries at the beginning of the phone conversation, the person on the other end may wonder why you're calling. Give that information right away.

It's always safe to ask, "Did I catch you at an okay time?" I recommend this phrase rather than "Did I catch you at a bad time?" because realistically, until you know this person well enough and he makes the decision that he wants to talk with you, if he's a busy person, any time you call will probably be a bad time. Until the person decides he wants to make time to talk with you, the best that you can hope for is to catch him at an okay time.

Be sure to smile when you use the phone. A person can hear a smile. They can also hear you typing on your keyboard so if you're on a phone call, be present and focused on the phone call. Much like when we communicate in person, the subtle messages we send over the phone can outshine our words.

## CONFERENCE CALLS

Conference calls are popular and time-efficient ways to communicate with several people at once. As a word of caution, unless you're speaking, activate the mute button. It's distracting when you hear all the multitasking that's happening in the background. Covering the phone with your hand while talking with someone else, coughing, going to the facilities, or typing on your computer is not enough. It can all be heard by others on the conference call unless your phone is muted.

The same goes for webinars. When a technology that uses webcams is being used, be aware if yours is activated.

## MOBILE DEVICES

Mobile devices are great conveniences as well as great distractions. As difficult as it is to lose touch with the outside world, turn off your cellphone and e-mail capabilities while you're at business functions. You're not hiding anything by doing the "BlackBerry prayer" under the table. Everyone knows you're typing a message to someone outside the room. Focus on the present moment and connect with the people who are in front of you.

Talking on mobile devices in any public location can be annoying to those around you. I've heard incredible life sagas while grocery shopping and waiting in restaurants. Is this really the message you want to be sending to random bystanders?

## TIMELINESS

Time is money. So, wasting people's time is equivalent to wasting their money. Earning a reputation as the person who is always late is undesirable. It sends the message that you are disorganized and that you disrespect other people and their time.

Be sure to schedule enough time in between appointments to accommodate the unexpected. Jamming too much into too short a period of time can run you ragged and make you less effective.

As a courtesy when running late, call or e-mail the person to indicate you'll be delayed in getting to the meeting.

If you are going to be late by 10 minutes or more, you definitely have to call to keep your contact from wondering if you've forgotten. After waiting for 15 minutes, without notification of your late arrival, it is acceptable for your contact to leave.

## SCHEDULING AND CANCELLING APPOINTMENTS

Whenever possible, cancel appointments a minimum of 48 hours in advance. Professionals who live by their calendar would have scheduled other appointments and possibly travel plans around your agreed-upon meeting time. Notify the other person as soon as you realize you are no longer available at that time. Whenever possible, stick to the time that was scheduled. When people are traveling from out of town, do whatever you can to not change the appointment time, as it can have a domino effect on the rest of their travel plans.

## HOW TO SAY NO WITHOUT BURNING A BRIDGE

For a word we hear so often in our lives, no is difficult to say when we're asked to do something, especially in the professional realm. Saying yes all the time means you're going to run out of time, money, and energy, which are limited resources.

The worst way to say no is to not respond to requests. It's unprofessional to leave someone hanging, hoping he will conclude that because you're ignoring him, you're not interested. You'll feel uncomfortable the next time you see the person and rightly so. To ignore someone is just short of being ignorant.

> ## To ignore someone is just short of being ignorant.

People are adults. Sure they may be disappointed, but their world will not crumble if you do not join the committee, come over for dinner, or buy their product.

The first step in learning how to say no is to decide when you want to say yes. Activities that fit your focus board (See Chapter 63: Finding Your Focus) make great "yes" opportunities. Decide if you have the time and financial resources to follow through and if so, great. Say yes.

If the answer must be no, here is a simple way to say no without offending others. This example would be useful if you were asked and weren't able to join a board of directors or committee. If this doesn't match your personality, use the premise of this technique, but tone it down so it is genuine for you and applicable to your situation.

"Am I ever flattered, honored in fact, that you would think of me for such an important role. That being said, after looking at my calendar and considering my current work and family commitments, I know I wouldn't do the role justice. I would hate to say yes, then not deliver. I'd make you look bad for recommending me. I hope you understand and can respect this decision."

You can also add (but only if it is truthful and applies to the situation): "Even though I am not able to assist in an official capacity, by all means, please keep me posted if there are upcoming events. I would be happy to buy a ticket or make a donation to support such a worthwhile cause."

You could also offer a recommendation in case the person doesn't know who else to ask. You could say, "I wonder if so-and-so would be in a better position to help you in this case. If you'd like, I'd be happy to make the introduction."

Now, if someone is asking you to sponsor him for a run, something this elaborate would not be necessary, but if you really don't wish to sponsor this person for any reason, take elements from this technique to politely say no. A simple, "Unfortunately, I've already allocated my donations for this year" will suffice.

## MEETINGS

Before any meeting, challenge yourself to determine if your attendance at the meeting is really necessary. Meeting-happy cultures within organizations can develop very quickly and can zap productivity.

If you are the one in charge of calling the meeting, don't have a meeting just for the sake of having a meeting. Make sure that before you ask others to attend, you have a full, substantial agenda, and that you are only inviting those who have a direct concern with the topics being discussed. Be clear and honest about the intention for the meeting so attendees can decide if it's a worthwhile time investment for them to attend.

Schedule an end time and respect it. There are few meetings that require longer than one hour to complete the agenda. If you find meetings are lasting longer, there may be too much focus on doing the work rather than deciding what work needs to be done and then delegating accordingly.

Before you speak at a meeting, jot down a list of the points you would like to make on a piece of paper. That will help you avoid pontificating. It's difficult for people to like you when you're holding up the meeting just to hear yourself talk. Short, sweet, and right-to-the-point comments make for effective meeting control.

As the chair of a meeting, take time to learn techniques that will ensure meetings are respectful of attendees and their time.

## CLOSING THE LOOP

When a person makes a recommendation or connects you with an individual, close the loop on the situation. Just a quick note, such as the following, will work: "Thanks for connecting me with so-and-so. We're going to meet on Monday to see if there is potential to collaborate" or "Thanks for the recommendation; she's a great accountant."

Tying up loose ends shows respect for the person who opened and shared his network with you. On a few occasions when I've set people up with potential employers, I didn't find out they got the job until months later. A quick update with the happy news would have gone a long way to solidifying our professional relationship.

It's also professional to keep people updated on progress if they've offered you assistance or support, whether it's sponsoring a cause, cheering you on as you look for work, or mentoring you as you start your career.

When you leave loops open it can be awkward. If you've ever avoided someone at an event because you were supposed to send them information or thank them for their generosity, then you know what I mean when I stress the importance of always closing the loop.

## SHOWING APPRECIATION

When someone goes above and beyond general expectations for you, it's only polite to thank him or her. Actually, whenever anyone does anything for you, it's appropriate to give thanks. The situation will dictate what should be done—use your judgment and match your personality to your response.

Every now and again, I'll meet with young professionals who act as if picking my brain and accessing my professional network are things to which they are entitled. I've talked with others who have noticed an increase in the same kind of attitude. This sense of entitlement is not appropriate because it does not encourage long-term, mutually beneficial business relationships.

After several attempts to connect one person with various employers, I realized that not once did he offer a simple thank you. In fact, each time I updated him on my efforts on his behalf, he simply asked for another favor and another connection. Despite his qualifications and positive in-person impression, his behavior deterred me from helping him further.

Failing to thank someone is a surefire way to stop the development of a relationship. Conversely, those who offer sincere appreciation make you feel good about helping them and you're more likely to continue on the same generous path.

A handwritten thank-you card is a lost art form, but one that is always noticed and appreciated. When people have made a tremendous impact on my life, I will opt to send them a gift basket that supports a local charitable cause or that has some neat goodies for people to share in the office.

When attending a dinner party at someone's home, it is appropriate to bring a host or hostess gift. A bottle of wine or flowers will suffice. Visit a specialty store for more unique gifts if it's a special occasion or you would like to stray from the norm. A follow-up thank-you call within 48 hours of a dinner party is a minimum pleasantry and a follow-up thank-you note is always appreciated.

## ALCOHOL

Know your limits. As much as you may think you can handle alcohol, it affects the brain's normal functioning. There are many business deals that have gone sideways thanks to an inappropriate comment made due to the influence of alcohol. Just because other people choose to drink does not give you the green light to do the same. It's better to stay in control than to risk doing something you'll regret.

### Getting drunk will not earn you points in the professional realm.

Limit alcohol to one or two drinks in public. Getting drunk will not earn you points in the professional realm. DO NOT drink and drive. Not only is this just a good personal policy, getting behind the wheel after drinking is irresponsible, inconsiderate, illegal, and will detract from your credibility. The price of a taxi is nothing compared to the potential damage mixing alcohol and driving could cause.

# Summary

---

## *The Third Pillar of Profitable Networking: Procedures*

- Mastering the fundamentals of networking will add to your professional image and give you confidence.
- A name tag should include your first and last names as well as company name. Place it high near your right shoulder.
- Your handshake is the subconscious communication of your character. Every handshake counts.
- Make a conscious effort to remember names by using the Shift, Listen, Solidify, and Think strategy.
- Accept the fact that people may forget your name. Kindly offer your first and last name to new and reacquainted contacts to ease the pressure of them trying to figure out who you are.
- Dining should be an enjoyable experience, not only for you, but for everyone around you as well. Be considerate of others.
- The attitude you bring to an event is as important as what you do when you are there.
- Make the most of your time at networking functions. Consider your cost for being in the room and be sure you are getting your money's worth.
- Educate your significant others and networking buddies about your goals and the path required to succeed so you can network effectively together.
- Don't underestimate the power of pre-event planning. A game plan for attendance at an event will give you purpose so you can maximize your time.

- Know the Mingling Formula: initiate dialogue, create a mini-bond, exchange contact information, move on, and repeat often.
- Be prepared to confidently engage in dialogue.
- Make a conscious effort to become an effective listener.
- Creating mini-bonds is vital to networking. Without them, connections won't deepen.
- Adopt a business-card system that works for you. Show respect when accepting cards by reading the information in front of the person who gave it to you.
- Develop your own 5-10-15-Second Communication so you can effectively answer the question "What do you do" in a mingling situation.
- Whatever your personality, you can tailor techniques to your comfort zone to maximize your networking.

# The Fourth Pillar of Profitable Networking

*Strategic Plan*

# 51

# Now What?

You have dealt with the Business of YOU. You are confident. You know the mechanics of networking, which means you're well-equipped to present a professional, put-together image that will inspire meaningful connections. Your attitude is on track and you're committed to giving the consistent effort required to create a profitable network.

Now what? Where do you need to go to meet the right people? Who are the "right" people? Once you meet them, what do you do to transition those casual business-card contacts into worthwhile business relationships?

Regardless of how professional and polished your image is and how well you can deliver all the elements of networking, if you don't put yourself in positions to use them, you're not going to grow your network. Talking about networking and actually networking are two different things.

## Talking about networking and actually networking are two different things.

It is amazing how people will say they want to build their network, but then a month later they still haven't gone to an event or made an effort to connect with key contacts. Bottom line: if you want to expand your network, then you have to network.

Networking takes work. As we established earlier, it takes six months or as many as six to eight casual encounters before you'll hit someone's radar screen and start to lower the natural trust barrier. You can lower the number of interactions required by deepening the intensity of each exchange. For example, you'll make more of an impression by having a solid, nonconfrontational conversation about politics or your plans for business growth than you will by having another superficial conversation such as "Hi, how are you?" "Good. Busy. How are you?" "Yeah, me too. Good. Busy." Of course, deeper conversations need to be handled in a way that is appropriate and nonthreatening.

In about six months you'll start to notice a comfort level in a group and should start to see some profits materializing from your efforts. With consistent and persistent effort, you will have a solid foundation for your network and should know whomever you need to know to make whatever you need to make happen, happen.

That requires focus and a clear understanding of what you want to accomplish and who you need to meet. The alternative to the strategic approach is the "throw-mud-on-the-wall-and-hope-something-sticks" technique. While this is popular, it is the reason so many people spin their wheels without seeing the desired return on investment.

The goal is to put yourself in a position to win. With limited time and money, why not use those resources to be at the right events with the right people who are likely to result in connections that will lead to business?

# 52

## The Logical First Step

THE MOST LIKELY STARTING POINT to build a profitable network is to analyze your current network and figure out who you already know. If you have networked for years, or if you're brand new to the concept, chances are you already have a solid base of contacts available to jump-start your networking efforts. You may just not realize it. Think of your friends, your family, your family's friends, your work colleagues, or your teammates as a start.

When we talk about networking we automatically assume that we need to go out to meet new people even though you're likely sitting on opportunities hidden within your current network and you've just not tapped into its potential yet.

Imagine that for every day you're alive, you've crossed paths with three new people. Some days there are more, such as when you're in school, start a new job, or go to a friend's party, whereas some days there are fewer, such as when you're home sick or were an infant. For easy numbers, let's say three is about right. For those who are more outgoing it could be more, for those who are shy, it could be less. So, 3 × 365 days a year is 1,095 people. We'll round down to roughly 1,000 new interactions per year.

By that calculation, if you are 33 years old, you have encountered approximately 33,000 people. Someone 55 years old would have encountered 55,000 people and so on. It's not likely that you can name that many people. Even cut the number by a half or a third and it's still a stretch.

Those of you who are not already using a data-management system should start by compiling a list of everyone you know into one accessible electronic tracking system. As you gather these names, don't restrict who goes on the master list. Think about the number of people you've met in your lifetime. For how many of these contacts could you find phone numbers, plus street or e-mail addresses with a moment's notice? If the answer is not many, this activity will change that.

## Are you surrounding yourself with people who influence you positively or negatively?

Once your master list is complete, review it. Ask yourself, "How can my current network help me achieve my goals and aspirations? Have I attracted the kind of people I want into my life?" By simply taking time to consider your list and your current circles of influence, you may notice a pattern. Are you surrounding yourself with people who influence you positively or negatively? While not everyone in your network will specifically impact your business or career growth goals, if you don't have the people who can, then you need to be aware of that and work toward creating some advantageous relationships.

Next, check your list to find the most successful person on it. Does this successful person know you too? If yes, that's great! This is where and with whom your official business networking efforts will begin.

Put a smile on your face and call that person. Let him or her know you want to get more involved in the community or that you are looking for a new job. Perhaps you have just started a new job and want to build your network.

Whatever your needs are, be up front about your intention for making the initial contact and setting the meeting. It may help if you say, "You're the most successful person I know, so I thought I would start by calling you. I'm really hoping to build my business network and I would be interested to hear how you got started and see if you have any ideas for me."

There are many reasons to start your networking plan by reaching out to the most successful people you know. It will stretch you out of your comfort zone early in the process and, therefore, make all of your subsequent networking efforts easier.

As you build your network, you will need to find a mentor who will take you under his or her wing to help you get established. Launching yourself with the movers and shakers from the beginning will give you credibility and start your networking efforts on a high-end, positive note. It's more advantageous to be sent down the influence chain than it is to try to gain credibility in the upward direction. The highest level of influence to which you have access is the current "top" of your circle of influence. That's the ideal place to find a mentor. Aim too low and you may not gain the insights and clout you're looking for to make an impact. However, if you aim too high and ask someone to be your mentor who represents too much of a gap between success and personality alignment, then you'll be disappointed because they won't nurture you the way you want.

Still, you need to start the outreach process with the most successful people you know and who also know you. Whether or not these initial conversations grow into mentorship opportunities is irrelevant at this point. The goal is to gain some insights and the lay of the networking land in your community and ideally in your profession. As you have these conversations, keep the mentor search in the back of your mind. It could very well be this first person you call, but don't be discouraged if it's not. Finding the right fit for a mentor is a process all on its own.

### You can't learn how to become successful from someone who is unsuccessful.

Surround yourself with people who have achieved what you want to achieve. This way you'll be motivated, mentored, and ready to succeed. You can't learn how to become successful from someone who is unsuccessful, whereas those who have surpassed your current success will inspire you and show you the way.

When you call your most successful person of choice, it's important to already have a connection with him (or her) through a mutual friend or family member. It is actually best if you've met personally before. That way, when you call, he will have a reference point for who you are and will be happy to speak with you. Hopefully, he will point you in the right direction to help you start your networking process.

If your relationship is strong enough to go for lunch or breakfast, then ask for that. If not, ask to meet either in his office or by phone for 15 to 20 minutes maximum, so the timeline is short and convenient. Let him know you would like to learn how to create success and emulate what he has done. This outlines the purpose of the meeting and gives the person an opportunity to agree to it or not. Make sure you respect the time limit by not staying longer than you promised.

When you meet, be on time and be prepared. Be honest and open about your ideal vision as determined in Chapter 2. Ask questions and seriously listen to the answers. Take a pen and paper to write brief notes.

Let the conversation flow. You will learn more by listening than by talking. After all, he's the expert and you are the student. Know in advance what you want to learn during this meeting and prepare some relevant questions. However, avoid turning the meeting into an interrogation interview.

It's natural to be a little nervous when you're sitting in front of the one you deem to be the most successful person you know, but remember, this person has already agreed to meet with you. Relax and enjoy the experience.

As you build your network, and especially in these mentorship-type settings, there are two vital questions that will help you expand your network:

1. Where should I go?
2. Whom should I meet?

Asking your contacts these questions will give you the direction you need to connect the dots to create a profitable network. Their answers will give you valuable insight that you can use to develop your overall plan. Caution: even if they give you good ideas, you need to check them against your focus board (See Chapter 63: Finding Your Focus) and be sure they make sense for you. Despite the best intentions, well-meaning advice is usually based on a narrow understanding of your overall larger plan.

In a best-case scenario, here is how these types of meetings will unfold. This is exactly how I got my start in the community, my first job as a fundraiser, and have helped others get connected. Obviously, the scenario is different for everyone.

For example, imagine you're a young professional who wants to find a job in the technology sector. You call the most successful person you know, who just happens to be the gentleman whose lawn you cut all the way through high school. He is the chief executive officer of an oil and gas company.

You did a great job for him all those years, so he already perceives you as reliable. You walk into the meeting presenting a professional image. You're prepared, punctual, and looking polished in your tidy suit.

At your meeting, you explain your ideal job and the type of company you want to work for in the technology sector. You ask, "Is there anywhere you think I should go or anyone you think I should meet?"

Mr. CEO ponders for a moment and calls his colleague to ask what technology show it was that she mentioned her husband was going to on the weekend. He explains to her that he has a young person sitting in his office who is looking for a job in technology.

Since the CEO and his colleague have a positive relationship through networking, she trusts his judgment and she agrees to introduce you to her husband, who happens to own a technology company. He may not be hiring, but at least you will gather information about the technology show and he can introduce you to others who are potentially hiring.

That's how networking can work, but to make a ripple effect like that happen, you need to take responsibility to identify and approach people you perceive to be successful and potentially significant in your life so you can ask the key questions. If you don't ask, people won't think to give you the answers.

## If you don't ask, people won't think to give you the answers.

You can repeat the process with more than one person, but start with the most successful choice and then work toward your honorable mentions.

There is no limit to the number of times you can use this approach to make connections. However, each time follow these six equally important rules:

1. Contact people with whom you already have a connection, either on your own or through a mutual contact.
2. Respect their time: keep your meetings brief, be prepared, and be clear about your intentions.
3. Follow up on their suggestions, otherwise their time was wasted. Lack of follow-up is the most common mistake professionals make.
4. Don't pressure them to connect you with their network on the spot. Recognize that some professionals aren't as forthcoming when it comes to sharing their contacts—and rightly so. They've spent years building trusting relationships and expanding their circles of influence. That should not be taken lightly.
5. Thank them for the time spent with you. Remember, people don't have to meet with you; they choose to.
6. Keep them posted on your progress, especially if the good news you have to share is a result of their guidance.

There you have it—your first step in building a profitable network. Connect with the most successful person(s) you know and see where these connections lead you. Even if you've been networking for a while, this is a great way to engage your current network and boost your results to the next level.

# 53

## Electronic Filing System

To tap into your professional network, information about your contacts needs to be easily accessible. This requires an electronic filing system. Old-fashioned paper address books won't cut it in today's competitive world and nor do online social networking sites count as an actual professional database.

A client prided herself on her business-card filing system. She had hundreds of cards filed alphabetically in a leather-bound business-card book. I agreed that her system looked very impressive.

During a consulting session, she mentioned her plans to contact a certain fellow when the company was ready to open its next satellite office. It was a commendable plan, but when asked about the contact she couldn't remember his name, only the country where he lived. After flipping through pages of business cards, she found a card she thought might be his, but she wasn't sure.

If this client had been using an electronic filing system and had included all pertinent details in the notes section, she simply could have searched for her potential contact by referencing his country and the project name. In a matter of seconds, her computer would have produced a short list of people from his country who were associated with the project.

This client gets bonus points for making an effort to organize her business cards because often professionals will not organize them at all. It's normal for me to visit offices where I see stacks of business cards bound with elastic bands or cards thrown randomly in a desk. These systems—or lack thereof—don't allow for effective relationship management.

# There's a difference between having a bunch of business cards and having a strong network of meaningful contacts with easily accessible contact information.

There's a difference between having a bunch of business cards and having a strong network of meaningful contacts with easily accessible contact information.

Those of you who have not been tracking contacts electronically have a big task ahead. If you did not complete your master list of contacts when it was suggested in the last chapter, now is the time to compile all of their information into one database.

Those who type slowly or who lack the time to input the data should hire someone to do it for you. It will be money well spent.

Regardless of which program you use, you'll want to track all pertinent details about each contact. The cellphone, a popular electronic storage device, is not a substitute for a real contact-management system, nor are social media sites. Always be sure to include any notes about the person in your electronic filing system. The type of system you use depends on your budget and your tracking needs. I use Outlook, but others use more elaborate systems like Sage Act and SalesForce.com databases.

I wish I had learned that trick when I started networking. There are countless people whom I've met along the way, yet I have no idea how to reach them now, nor do I remember how we met. It wasn't until a few years after I started exchanging business cards that I realized the unequivocal importance of a proper system to track contacts.

You can import Facebook and LinkedIn (or any other online social networking portal) contacts into your master list. This is helpful because you want to be able to access their contact details quickly and keep them on your business-development radar screen. There will be contacts who are just online contacts and who don't necessarily belong in your database. Your electronic system should be an accurate reflection of your network. If you wouldn't recognize them offline, then don't include them in your master list.

Once all your business-card information is entered into your data system, proceed to the next chapter to review and categorize your contacts. Don't forget to back up your list of contacts.

# 54

## Categorizing Contacts

TO TAP INTO THE POWER OF NETWORKING, you must first be aware of who is in your network and how they impact your strategic plan. You've just made a master list of everyone you know. Now figure out where those people fit in your professional life. It's really difficult to manage relationships with absolutely everyone you know, so I've found categorizing contacts is helpful.

This becomes increasingly important as the number of people in your network grows. It's also extremely important if you have collected a lot of business cards over the years and most of your contacts have no relevance in your life.

A client had close to 750 names in his electronic database yet he insisted he didn't have anywhere to start his networking and business-development efforts. So I asked him to review and categorize all 750 names.

At our next meeting, the number of his legitimate contacts dropped to almost 150. The other 600 names were of people he didn't know or remember. They were mostly the result of cold calls he made at the start of his investment career. Some were random business cards he'd entered, but he couldn't remember anything about the people represented by the cards, so they weren't considered meaningful contacts.

The exercise gave us a manageable place to start. In addition to eliminating all the people who weren't really contacts, the exercise identified priority prospects with whom he'd forgotten to follow up concerning their investment portfolios.

## The more people you have in your database, the more important it is to organize your current network.

The more people you have in your database, the more important it is to organize your current network. Otherwise it will be difficult to grasp the complexity of your network and tap into it effectively. Online networking sites can expand your network significantly, making this categorization process even more overwhelming.

The reason we're categorizing your contacts is so you can create a relationship-management action plan for each category. When time and networking resources are tight, you can focus on the priorities within your system.

As you review your current list and add new contacts to it, you'll want a system that allows you to categorize each contact easily. Without an easy-to-use system, you run the risk of just collecting names, rather than keeping them organized enough to generate long-term mutually beneficial business relationships.

Eventually you'll set specific expectations for yourself for how you stay in contact with each category and manage the relationship flow. Therefore, the more straightforward you make your contact categorization system, the more likely you will be to follow it.

Please note: this list is your actual network, not a database that you've acquired online or people who have subscribed to your newsletter. These are people you're connected to and who you would recognize if you saw them.

Adapt the categories so they make sense for your situation. The minimum number of categories should be three, the maximum should be five.

1. General Contacts
2. Connectors
3. Target Market
4. Clients
5. Random Names

This system helps determine action steps for further connection and ongoing relationship management. For those involved in multiple projects, subcategories within each of the categories may be helpful to track people who apply to different industries or projects in which you're involved. Just don't get too complicated. Choosing too many categories can make your database too cumbersome, thereby making it difficult to implement on an ongoing basis. Then chances are your use of it will fizzle. The idea is to make a fast judgment about the next steps for follow-through and relationship management for each contact. If you only have three to five categories in your database system, a decision as to where a new contact belongs becomes easy, fast, and accurate for successful retrieval when needed.

Once you've established the categories you'll use to manage your contacts, print a master list of your current contact database. One by one, go through the list to assign a category to each contact. Once that's complete, then we'll move them through the corresponding relationship-development action plan in the next chapter. During this process consider the needs of those in your network. What is happening in their lives right now? Are they buying a new car or a new home? When you listen to and actually think about the people you know, you'll be surprised how much information about them you have already stored in your head.

As you perform this exercise, you may find natural connections. For example, you may know that your friend Sue is looking for a new babysitter and that Sandra's daughter just finished her babysitting course. Why not connect the two? They'll be thankful you did.

## 1. GENERAL CONTACTS

These are the people you meet, but who don't seem to have a specific place in your professional network yet. An immediate connection was not established. They are not identified as potential clients nor have specific reasons for follow-up been identified. These are miscellaneous contacts, family, friends, and former colleagues who have no current business relevance for you. People in the general category will likely form the bulk of your network.

Keep notes about each person as we discussed in previous chapters. I often look to my general contacts to connect other people with services.

**As circumstances evolve, general contacts and connectors may become part of your target market category.**

These contacts are as important to track as those in the next categories because you never know what the future may hold. People who start in your database as general contacts may change categories as your paths cross and circumstances evolve.

## 2. CONNECTORS

For me, as will be the case for you, these contacts are the pulse of my network. Our personalities click. We share common goals and perhaps we plan to collaborate on projects or community initiatives.

These are the movers and shakers of the present or possibly the future. Formal and informal mentors usually fall into this category. Connectors are happy to connect others and are happy to connect with you. They are part of your circle of influence and create the core of your business network. These could be the favorites who are both friends and business contacts. Blurring the business and friendship boxes is easiest in this category.

Perhaps your services are complementary and sending referrals to each other seems likely. Developing relationships with people in this category is enjoyable because you like them, trust them, and believe they are competent, and vice versa. As well, these relationships could prove to be professionally advantageous and profitable someday.

Focus on nurturing long-term relationships with this group. Think of the connectors as individuals you won't necessarily do business with today (although you may), but as the people who will lead you to business tomorrow. Money may never change hands, but they could open doors for you and you could open doors for them.

## 3. TARGET MARKET

These are the people who have been identified or who have identified themselves as potential clients or priority professional relationships. They need timely follow-up and should move to the top of your priority list to start the sales process. As circumstances evolve, general contacts and connectors may become part of your target-market category. This doesn't have to be all sales focused. Building relationships in the media or with specific philanthropists may be a priority as well.

When you're trying to fill your networking calendar, look to this list to see whom you could connect with again. Before you go to events, you can review this list and see who in your target market is likely to attend. If you don't know them well enough, consider your connectors to see if any of them are associated to people in your target-market and subsequently could put in a good word for you. When you do your pre-event homework, you may consider the people from your target-market list who will be in the room. At times when you are looking to book sales meetings, you can pull a list of prospects from your target market and take appropriate steps to move them closer to being actual clients.

## 4. CLIENTS

This is a pretty obvious category. Once you've earned their business you'll want to be sure to stay in touch with your clients to develop deeper relationships that generate loyalty.

## 5. RANDOM NAMES

This is a tentative category. Much like the story about the advisor with 750 names in his database but with only 150 actual contacts, most databases need to be purged. Names from cold-call lists may have crept into your database. In the short term, you can file them under "random names" and once you're done reviewing your list, make a decision as to what you're going to do with these strangers.

Can they legitimately move to your target-market list? If so, how can you do that? Or, is it better to clear the clutter and delete them from your master list?

As you meet new contacts, it will take less time to monitor and categorize where they fit into your network. If you categorize contacts automatically when you get a new business card and keep up to date with inputting data, this process will happen very quickly and smoothly. Add a "category" tab to your electronic database so contacts can be easily sorted and managed according to your categories.

## THE IMPORTANCE OF CATEGORIZING CONTACTS

You can't push a marshmallow into a piggy bank. No matter how hard you try, an unmelted marshmallow just won't squish through the slot.

Trying to push a general contact into the target-market category before he is a qualified prospect will generate the same frustration for both of you. So will asking a general contact to send you a referral before trust has been established or a business relationship has been developed between the two of you.

> **Recognizing where people fit in your network will keep you from taking the wrong approach to building relationships.**

Recognizing where people fit in the grand scheme of your profitable network will keep you from jumping the gun and taking the wrong approach to building relationships. In the future, connectors are likely to become clients or they may send referrals to you, but establishing this comfort level and mutual trust takes time.

# 55

---

# Relationship-Development Action Plan

ONCE YOU'VE CATEGORIZED your contacts and have a good sense of the people you know, you'll need a game plan to take these relationships to the next level. Your categorization system will determine the key people with whom you need to connect and the best course of action to move those contacts to the next level.

## GENERAL CONTACTS

Since these are people you've indicated are not relevant in your professional realm at this time there is no specific ongoing plan of action required other than to loosely stay in touch. Some will be people you'll just run into naturally. Your friends will just continue on the natural relationship path that made them your friends in the first place. Just keep that going.

The only caution about this group is that you don't want to lose touch completely. If there are people you won't cross paths with at least a few times a year as you go about your life, then you need to find some way to stay visible to them. Christmas cards, random catch-up phone calls, and summer BBQs are simple strategies. Social media can also play a huge role in staying connected. Read their status updates and comment on them as well as share relevant comments on your profiles.

Inevitably, circumstances will change and suddenly you'll need to reach out to the people with whom you've lost touch. Once you need a new job or change careers and want their business, it's more awkward to contact them. We've all had the phone calls, "Hi, I know we haven't talked in 15 years, but

I'm an investment advisor and I wonder if you'd like me to take care of your portfolio."

It's so much easier if you stay on each other's minds on an ongoing basis. Then, when you need to ask for a job or a lead, your contact with this person doesn't come out of the blue.

## CONNECTORS

These are your most important professional relationships. They are the go-to people in your community/profession, your mentors, and the ones who can open doors to opportunity. While they may include your favorite clients, it's not necessarily a client/supplier relationship and if it is, that is not necessarily the focus of conversation when you're networking together.

When you talk with them, the tone is one of finding mutually beneficial scenarios and moving ideas forward. True connectors make introductions for you once they've decided they are on your side. It is essential that they like you, trust you, and believe you're competent before they'll open their network to you.

At minimum you want to have a one-on-one meaningful interaction with these people twice a year, and ideally, once a quarter. This means sharing a meal together, talking during a private in-office meeting, a sports outing, or something else of mutual interest that can deepen the relationship.

In addition to meaningful one-on-one time approximately every quarter, you'll want to run into them in a group or casual capacity about once a month. You never want more than six weeks to go by without some connection. This could be seeing each other at a charity event or networking function, or by way of a phone call or e-mail. This is an opportunity to stay on their radar screen and solidify the association, but not necessarily deepen the relationship.

One way you can help each other is to clearly understand what the other person needs in order to move forward in their business. After you've earned the mutual trust and respect, then when you want to get in front of prospects, and your connector knows them, you can ask for an introduction. Be careful to ask for a reasonable number of connections. Nothing drains a relationship faster than one person continuously riding the coattails of others. Even though the connector may be willing to open doors, it's still up to you to develop the relationships and build your own profitable network. Some relationships take years to nurture and that process can't be taken lightly.

It's better to ask for two highly influential introductions a year rather than a whole bunch of favors every time you see someone. You'll quickly earn a reputation as a taker if you ask for too much, are too demanding, or never reciprocate.

If you want to meet more of your connectors' contacts, then go with them to networking outings and the introductions will naturally occur. When you know you're going to be at the same event together, you can even give them advance notice that you're hoping to meet so-and-so and then they can introduce you at the function. A quick introduction while you happen to be in the same room cashes in less goodwill currency than asking someone to pick up the phone and make an introduction as a specific task.

Connectors are powerful relationships, but only if there is a sense of reciprocity. The power is in mutually beneficial business relationships. You may not be able to contribute in the same way or to the same depth. For example, your connectors may already have significant contacts and thus may not be looking to you for access to your less influential network. Therefore, you need to "earn your keep" in some other way such as supporting your connector's favorite charitable cause or offering insights in your area of expertise. Perhaps explaining how social networking works, including them in an adventure they wouldn't normally have, or simply by bringing joy to their lives are options that can all contribute to the goodwill account.

## TARGET MARKET

Ultimately, this is your list of prospects who need to move into the sales process or perhaps they already are in your revenue funnel. The goal of the sales process is for you to move people into the client, connector, or general categories rather than have them stay as a prospect forever. A name that never becomes a yes or no will drive you crazy and keep you from being profitable. A no is better than an imaginary maybe. Pick up the phone, ask the right questions, and make success happen.

If you've identified someone as being in your target market, there must be a reason. Somehow you must perceive that they have a problem for which you could provide the solution.

There are two types of people in a target market or prospect list: suspects and prospects. It's important to recognize the difference. When I sit down with advisors and ask about their prospect list, it's often merely a list of suspects.

Here's the difference: A suspect is someone you think would make a great client. A prospect is someone who would agree with you. That means they at least have to know who you are, what you do, and if asked, would most likely sit down with you to discuss business. When we separate our target market and potential clients with this suspect versus prospect mind-set it makes it easier to predict our sales growth and the likelihood of closing a sale.

There are countless books that talk about the sales process. This book is focused on the networking process, which is not selling. Networking will get you the introduction, but at some point you have to actually talk business, make a sales pitch, and determine if there is a fit for you to work together.

Figure out what your sales process is once you meet someone who identifies as a target market. For me, it's really simple. The majority of my business has come from conversations over a lunch meeting or at a networking event when a person who is a decision maker—or could introduce me to the decision maker—for a target client expressed an interest in my training content. That meant all I had to do was present the options for training their team—such as workshops, conference keynotes, technology-driven virtual training, or a large-scope consulting program for their entire firm. Then I keep following up until they make a decision as to how they would like to engage my services.

## RANDOM NAMES

These names definitely fall under the "suspects" category. The majority of the time the best way to deal with this list is to delete it. If there is no connection and it's just a cold list, the best you can do is to find a way to warm it. Consider, perhaps, a phone campaign or direct-mail piece that includes a link to a relevant website or introductory video—something to entice people to take notice of how your service would be valuable.

**If there is no connection and it's just a cold list, the best you can do is to find a way to warm it.**

Short of that, there isn't much hope for the list. The reason this category exists, as mentioned above, is to give you a temporary resting place for these names until you decide what you're going to do with them. The sooner you take action to either delete the name or move it into a warm category, the sooner you can focus on nurturing your real-life network of people you know and who know you.

# 56

## Following Up

THE IMPORTANCE OF THE FOLLOW-UP should be a given. We're always told we need to follow up and yet the follow-up rate is dismal. We don't need to recite alarming business statistics to know just how bad follow-up is among networkers. Just think of the last networking event you attended and how few people actually contacted you as promised after the event. Consider all of the "Let's do lunches" you have circling in the universe that will never land on a table and it's easy to recognize that this a missing ingredient in the professional realm.

In fact, ineffective follow-up is the main reason people don't develop a profitable network. Not only is follow-up required to create a relationship beyond the introductory pleasantries, it's what builds credibility and breaks down trust barriers.

There are several reasons we don't follow up. Among them are that we forget what we promised to do; after the event, we return to our lives that are already too busy and we don't make time; or we don't know how to do it.

### We're always told we need to follow up and yet the follow-up rate is dismal.

None of these are reasonable excuses. Set aside time each week to catch up on follow-ups and make it a priority on your calendar.

No one is perfect. From time to time, we all forget conversations and passing promises made, but aim for at least an 80 percent follow-up success rate and you will change your networking results drastically.

Here are some simple guidelines for follow-through and then we'll dive into strategies that apply to each category.

- Identify the people with whom you'd like to connect further.
- Identify the best reason to connect again.
- Plant the seed for the follow-up when you're in front of the person.
- Execute as promised.

Manage the various touch points, recognizing that just because you send one follow-up e-mail doesn't mean you have a relationship. Each category requires a different tone of follow-up to have the most success. This is why it's important to be able to easily and quickly categorize contacts.

Find a way to remind yourself that you promised follow-ups immediately after an event. For example, create a small dog-ear in the person's business card to indicate a follow-up is required or keep a mental tally of follow-ups. ("Okay, that's the second follow-up I promised.") At the end of the event, if you counted to five, it'll force you to retrace your steps and your conversations to remind you what you promised to do.

This is actually just good networking practice, regardless of follow-ups, when it comes to conversations or new contacts. "I met seven new people" or "That's my twentieth conversation tonight."

With all follow-ups, the easiest and most effective ones are those that are expected. Therefore, set the stage for the follow-up during in-person conversations. Not only does this apply to initial introductions and interactions at networking events but also it's an effective technique to use each time you talk with someone. Dropping hints about something you'll do next will keep the relationship moving forward, as you'll always have a reason to reconnect.

If you drop a "next step" in the middle of a meeting then it's implied that this isn't the last time you'll be connecting. Becoming a master at following up does take some effort, but it's a skill that will separate you from your competition.

The majority of your follow-ups will include a traditional e-mail or phone call. From there, depending on the mini-bond and your philosophy for online networking, you would want to connect online as well.

## GENERAL CONTACTS AND FOLLOW-UP

Any communication with this group is about strengthening the connection in hopes of eventually moving them to the connector or target-market category.

A common error that occurs is people follow up with casual general contacts with the same gusto as if they were connector or target-market contacts—for example, trying to send a sales or referral e-mail rather than a "look forward to seeing you again" e-mail. Here's an example of a follow-up e-mail modeled after this detrimental, albeit far-too-common, approach:

"It was great to meet you last night. I am attaching my marketing materials. If you happen to know anyone who needs my services, I would appreciate any referrals you could send my way. Likewise, if I hear of anyone looking for an (insert profession here) I will be happy to send them to you."

Really? Why would you be happy to do this? On what grounds are you basing the single greatest business compliment ever—the act of sending someone a referral?

Those who send and receive referrals know it happens naturally once a certain level of comfort and trust is established in relationships. Most importantly, on what grounds do you feel you have the right to ask this new acquaintance to refer you to others?

This technique reminds me of the relationship book *I Love You, Nice to Meet You* by Lori Gottlieb and Kevin Bleyer. If you make such significant gestures to practical strangers, you will appear insincere and you won't be setting yourself up for success.

After meeting someone briefly, a personalized e-mail that reflects the reality of your limited relationship yet opens the door for future dialogue is more appealing. For example:

"It was great to meet you last night at the event. Hopefully our paths will cross again. I'd like to get more involved in the community so if you hear of any other events you think may be worthwhile, by all means please let me know. By the way, if you run into our mutual friend, so-and-so, please give her my best."

While the first e-mail comes across as insincere, canned, and pushy, the second offers a genuine, nonthreatening attempt to keep in touch. It has a greater chance of making a long-term connection. At this point in the relationship, your e-mail signature indicating what you do through your company name and potentially your tag line will suffice. The welcoming content of your e-mail will help build the connection between the two of you, while your signature at the bottom of your e-mail will begin the education process as to what you do.

As you build your professional network, you will find a groove that works best for you. The key is to keep the process as natural as possible, matching your efforts with your personality.

## You don't need to follow up with everyone you meet.

You don't need to follow up with everyone you meet. Contacts in your general category usually don't require any immediate contact unless you are specifically hoping to move them into the target-market or connector category. However, take notice of those in your general contact list. Make a mental note to remember them the next time you connect.

As you learn more about your casual contacts, you may realize they belong in another category and you'll naturally develop a more intense professional connection. For example, you may send the simple follow-up e-mail and they may respond by saying they'd like to have a coffee or introduce you to someone who is looking for what you supply.

You never know, perhaps the next time you run into each other, your general contact may introduce you to someone in his network who will become a target-market contact for you.

Online networking resources are incredibly helpful for follow-ups. If there wasn't a reason to connect again or you're not quite sure how this connection could develop into a deeper professional relationship, you can turn to online portals. This will help you stay connected and learn more about them through their updates and profile. You can genuinely forge a relationship by commenting and engaging online, making the next time you see each other in person more familiar.

## CONNECTORS AND FOLLOW-UP

Following up with potential connectors is a priority. This reconnection takes a different tone than for general contacts and those who are moving into the sales process. The purpose is to create a long-term relationship, not to sell your product or charge for your service.

Ideally, a reason to follow up is determined during your face-to-face encounter. Once you've already agreed to coffee, lunch, or a phone call, then the follow-up is easy. Contact the person within a reasonable amount of time to make arrangements for the meeting to happen. If you wait longer than two business days to follow up, your contact may forget what the two of you agreed to do.

The same time guideline applies if someone offered to connect you or give you advice. A common mistake people make is failing to follow through on generous offers made by general contacts and connectors.

A person who offers to introduce you to someone or let you pick his brain usually means it. If he didn't genuinely mean it, but you follow up anyway, he is technically on the hook to help you. Most likely, you will earn respect by calling him. This person now knows that you are someone who should be taken seriously and who takes others at their word.

I introduced a good friend to a very successful businessman. At the time, my friend, although successful in his own right, was looking to change his career path to create a more fulfilling lifestyle. The businessman, who had made a similar transition years earlier, gave my buddy his card and offered to help. It was obvious he had a lot of relevant wisdom to share and was genuinely interested in sharing it. Unfortunately, my friend never took advantage of his offer.

Months later, the successful businessman and I ran into each other. He mentioned that my friend still hadn't called him. He then shared a story of another young professional to whom he made the same offer. Unlike my buddy, this fellow sent him an e-mail later the same night asking to book a meeting.

Which contact do you think is on track to building a professional relationship with this businessman? Both are equally talented and credible men, but one followed up—the other one did not.

### Those who have earned significant success are genuinely happy to help others achieve the same.

Those who have earned significant success are genuinely happy to help others achieve the same. Call it a pay-it-forward equivalent in the business world.

When a specific reason for follow-up has not been established, it may make sense to wait before making contact with a potential connector. Experience will help you determine the best rate for reconnecting. When in doubt, take a step back and look at the situation from a long-term perspective rather than focusing on the immediate returns.

Was there enough of a mini-bond established between the two of you so that when you call, he will remember who you are and want to pick up the phone? If not, when will you likely see this person again? Running into him a second and third time will establish more familiarity and will allow the relationship to build at a natural pace. Patience and perseverance are key elements.

If you sit on a committee together, depending on the dynamics of the group, it may make sense to wait a few meetings before making plans to connect one-on-one. Likely, an issue will arise that requires the two of you to meet, giving you an opportunity to get to know each other better. Allowing an appropriate pace for a connection to grow will strengthen the foundation for a long-term, mutually beneficial business relationship.

There are people with whom I rarely spend one-on-one time, yet they are still valuable members of my network. They are considered valuable members of my network because I know who they are, what they do, and what they have to offer, and I like them, trust them, and think they are competent, and vice versa. Sending these people referrals or picking up the phone when I have a quick question does not require an "official" networking meeting.

## TARGET MARKET AND FOLLOW-UP

A target-market contact has the highest priority in terms of follow-up and finding out if they are ready to move into the sales process. These are the people you've determined are a good fit for your product or service and have a connection with you.

Recently, I attended a political convention where I met a gentleman who is a partner in an international accounting firm. The conversation naturally led to what I have been doing since the end of my political campaign. Using the 5-10-15-Second-Communication approach (see Chapters 48 and 49), I explained that I had re-launched my company and was doing training and consulting on business networking.

By the end of my 15-second communication spot, he self-identified as wanting further information about my services for his firm's young-accountant-training program. I got his business card and that was the end of our business talk at the convention.

When I returned to my office, obviously he was a priority follow-up. Right away I sent him a personal note with a marketing package outlining the training workshops I could offer to his company. Weeks later I received a call from his human resources department to book a session.

This is an ideal-case scenario for turning casual business-card contacts into business relationships. I didn't have to "sell" my services; I just educated him on what services I offered. He did the "selling" inside his firm for me. The brief discussion (our entire conversation was no longer than five minutes) made this contact very easy to categorize as a target market. My appropriate course of action was very clear.

The firm had to hire someone for its training programs and now that I had connected with a senior-level partner, I had an advantage over my competition. All I had to do was follow through, as promised, after the convention.

Unfortunately, many professionals would fail to do this. If I had ignored his suggestion and not followed up, I wouldn't have been considered, let alone given the contract.

For the most part, this scenario reflects how I've built my entire company. It's also how I pursued donors during my career in the not-for-profit sector. I don't do cold calls and I don't try to sell my business services to people who don't want or need what I have to offer.

## A straightforward approach to follow up with contacts in your target market will earn you respect and a professional reputation.

A straightforward approach to follow up with contacts in your target market will earn you respect and a professional reputation. This is not the time to be wishy-washy or second-guess yourself, your product, or your services. You've already qualified the contacts as potential buyers so give them the opportunity to buy or use your services, not those of your competition.

When you move people into the sales process after an initial introduction, reference the reason you have identified them as a potential client.

For example: "Hi, Martha. Just following up from our conversation last night at the event. You mentioned you're looking for an accountant. As discussed, I am an accountant and would be pleased to meet with you to see if there's a fit. Here are some available dates: (insert dates). Let me know if any of those times work for you."

Simple, short, and to the point. There is no guess work. No hidden agenda, but there is an excellent opportunity to develop a business relationship. Provided you presented a genuine, welcoming professional image when you met, Martha should respond to your message. She has already identified that she is looking for your services, so the easier you make it for her to hire you, the more likely she will do that.

## 57

# Transitioning from Social to Business

EVER SINCE I STARTED MY TRAINING and consulting company, participants in my workshops have asked me how they can transfer their social networks into business. There are two scenarios that need to be addressed.

The first scenario is the one we discussed in Chapter 6 when your closest family and friends have put you in the friend box or pigeonholed you in another profession. For example, one day you're a bartender and the next you're a financial advisor. Or they can see you as a teacher, but not as a health and wellness expert.

The second scenario happens to all professionals regardless of what stage they are in in their careers and they often wonder how they can transfer social networks into business. The guys on the soccer team, the friends at the ski club, and the neighbors at the cottage represent huge opportunities in business. Finding the perfect rhythm to bridge the gap between social and business will be pivotal for you and the profitability of your network.

**Finding the perfect rhythm to bridge the gap between social and business will be pivotal for you and the profitability of your network.**

Let's tackle the first scenario. In order to change "boxes" you have three choices:

1. Make a bold transformation so they can't help but take notice. Arrive with a confident attitude, professionally groomed, and dressed like you're ready for business. Pair that professional image with taking your career seriously and they'll have to see something is different.
2. Prove them wrong. There is no greater game changer than walking the walk rather than just talking the talk. If someone isn't responding to you professionally, then just go find success elsewhere.
3. Address the hesitation specifically. The best and most professional way to approach this box change with friends is to address it. Let's imagine you're a financial advisor and you have buddies you've known since college who would make ideal clients. You could say:

"Listen, I know we're great friends and I never want to jeopardize that. As you know, I've stepped into this new role as a licensed financial planner. I am extremely committed to working with my clients and, obviously, I want the absolute best for my close friends and to be sure they are well taken care of with their financial plans. I know you're used to seeing me in our social settings, but I actually know what I'm doing when it comes to financial planning and would love to work with you. If we were to work together, I can assure you that your financial matters will remain strictly confidential and we would keep our business talk for times when it's appropriate to talk about business. What do you think? Do you want to sit down and see if there is a fit? At the very least, I can give you a second opinion and a fresh set of eyes on your finances to be sure you're on track to be sure the kids will have college funding."

This is the most long-winded preamble I'd ever recommend to ask someone to sit down to see if there's a fit for your services, but it's because you have to cover all the key objections that will restrict your close friends from wanting to jump into the client category:

1. Confidentiality. Sometimes people don't want to mix business with pleasure because they're worried others in their social circles may find out the details about their finances, health, or house renovations (whatever applies for you). Set them at ease by addressing privacy right up front.
2. Obligation. The best line I've found to set people at ease is "Let's see if there's a fit." To feel comfortable to move forward, they'll want to know that they can say no without feeling guilty.

3. Trust. They're concerned you're not competent and responsible. Highlight that even though you're social buddies there is more to you than playing cards on Saturday night.

4. Fear. They need to know you have their best interests in mind. Sharing that you are committed to serving clients and that you want to be sure they're taken care of shows you're looking to help them, not take them for granted.

5. Separation. They likely treasure your friendship and getaway time so set the stage that there will be boundaries so work will stay work and social encounters will stay social.

### If someone says no, they just aren't comfortable mixing business and pleasure. Respect that.

If they say no, they just aren't comfortable mixing business and pleasure. Respect that. Continue to serve your other clients and grow your business. In time, as you become even more successful, they may change their minds. If not, no problem; you still have a great friend.

What about the second scenario? How can your contacts from your R&R time impact your business growth results?

On one hand, there is an unwritten rule that no business is done at these hideaways, and yet, on the other hand, these are often the very people with whom you are most naturally aligned and who fit your target market as potential clients. Any time a group of like-minded people gather on the weekend at the golf club, the cottage, the ski hill, the tennis club, or any other social venue there is potential for business collaboration provided your supply and their demand align as well.

It doesn't have to be a difficult transition. You just need to learn a few approaches that will avoid the shoptalk on the beach, but still grow the shop.

Realize that people, you included, are at the cottage/club/hill to escape the usual grind of thinking about business, finances, responsibilities, and everything else that can cause stress. Respecting the need for downtime is imperative if you're going to turn these contacts into clients.

There is no doubt that business conversations will arise, but don't be the one to always initiate talk about business in social settings. Whatever you do, don't approach the conversation from a sales perspective; instead, come from a place of sharing information and creating interesting dialogue. Be aware of who is within earshot and be sure you're not boring others around you, including your spouse.

Use the social time to build genuine relationships. We're talking so much about how important it is to have strong, respectful relationships and here is a perfect chance to simply sit back, relax, and strengthen relationships away from the formalities of business. These are the genuine relationships that can be created over the long term, not just a quick hello at the next business function.

One of the fears of mixing business and pleasure is that once you cross the line there is no escaping these friends until you sell the cottage or stop going to the club. That means there is more pressure when you serve friends than when you work with people you only know professionally. As discussed in Chapter 6, in these circumstances there will be even more pressure on you to deliver.

Keep an eye on your alcohol consumption. Everyone is given a bit of slack in social settings; you just want to be sure that your loosened personality is aligned with your business personality. There is just no recovering from potential clients watching you eat crackers and pâté off the floor after you've tipped the tray in a tipsy tizzy.

The great part is that when there is a strong social relationship, if there is an alignment for a win-win business opportunity, then it will naturally present itself. People who have similar attitudes and values and run in the same circles together are bound to connect professionally as well.

As one business owner said to me, "If the synergies for working together with social friends don't come to the surface without having to be pushed, then you may be barking up the wrong tree. Just enjoy the friendship."

He's had success during weekends at his cottage by keeping conversations light. He focuses on creating solid friendships and defers the in-depth, professional talk to the work week when there is a possibility for business.

He recommends that the best time to bridge the gap between hanging out and doing business is the last time you'll see someone socially before they transition back to the work world (often on Sunday afternoon when everyone is packing up the boats). What seems to work best for him is a simple "It was great to see you this weekend. Let's talk this week about how we could do some business together." This seems to be the magic approach for him.

One thing for sure is that if you don't ask the question and transition from pleasure to business, then your cottage friends won't become your clients and that could hinder your profitable network.

# 58

# Maintaining Relationships

GREAT RELATIONSHIPS START WITH the basics. Get to know people, understand their needs, and learn what makes them tick. A genuine interest in others will make you likeable, will generate trust, and will create a foundation for future business opportunities and meaningful relationships.

As you expand your network and bring new associations into the fold, you'll want to ensure you maintain your current relationships. There are certain people whose relationships will be easier to sustain because you will interact with them on a regular basis. Among them are fellow committee members, key clients, and good friends.

It's the people on the periphery who require more deliberate attention. Find your own way to keep in touch with these people for nonbusiness-related purposes.

Often in networking, people will only call when they need something. Treasured relationships are developed in between the crunch times. If every time you call a contact it's because you need something, the natural back-and-forth development of the bond is hindered. This reactive attitude toward networking creates relationships that are about supply and demand rather than meaningful connections.

**A reactive attitude toward networking creates relationships that are about supply and demand rather than meaningful connections.**

Relationships will ebb and flow. There are times in the year when people are more active in the business community, whereas other times support a less intense pace.

For example, during the summer professionals still work, but there is a much less formal business environment as people take vacations and focus more on family. This is a perfect time to host a company's family picnic or invite people to participate in summer activities like golfing or boating.

Another strategy is to lunch every day with different people. There are some contacts who having lunch with once a year is enough to maintain a professional relationship. Throughout the year you will still interact at business functions or when pertinent issues arise, but planning some one-on-one time to catch up privately helps deepen the mini-bond.

Depending on the relationship, it may be necessary to have your "annual" lunch more frequently, perhaps every six months, once a quarter, or on a monthly basis depending on the circumstances. Early in the relationship you may need more frequent encounters and then it's just a matter of staying in touch through social media and bumping into each other every once in a while to solidify the relationship. Obviously if someone is a connector or a target market, this long interval in between personal visits isn't enough.

There are people who make a point to call others on their birthday. One friend is known as the guy who will call you on your birthday. For something that takes him about 10 minutes a day, it's a gesture that is usually appreciated and it gives him an excuse to make contact at least once a year. This kind of approach makes sense for some of your contacts, but I've also heard that it can be weird for people who don't know you that well to get a call on a day that is personal, so do what works best for you.

Another friend calls people to wish them a "happy anniversary" to mark their first lunch meeting together. This works well because it is a relevant date for the two of them.

Staying abreast of who is in your network and what's happening in their lives is a great way to stay connected. When someone you know is mentioned in the media, send them the clipping with a congratulatory note. This also applies to their family members. Recognizing their children's achievements can be equally gratifying.

When you plan to attend an event, send the notice to contacts you would like to get to know better. Perhaps you can pull together a table for the function. It's a great opportunity to play host and introduce other people as well. Just because you send the notice doesn't mean you have to pay for the tickets. Simply ask them to call the hosting organization to purchase their own tickets, saying they'd like to sit at your table. You can also mention the ticket price in your request. For example, "Tickets are $50 each, payable to the ABC Association." This implies that they are to pay their own way.

If an associate mentions a challenge they are having and a potential solution crosses your desk, feel free to forward the information. When someone is looking for a job or information, introduce him to someone in your network who could potentially help.

Reflect on your relationships. What is your natural rhythm for staying in touch with friends? Is there a way you could formalize that approach to make it a routine for more of your professional contacts?

# 59

## Tapping into Your Network

It's one thing to know a lot of people; it's another thing to be able to tap into those resources. People who network well establish a professional environment that encourages networking and collaboration. By networking with others, they set the stage for others to network with them. They've learned how to maximize the give-and-take roles that naturally occur in relationships.

The first requirement to tap into your network is to have a network established. If people don't know who you are, what you do, and what you have to offer, nor do they like you, trust you, and believe you are competent, you won't have a foundation from which to build.

Develop your network before you need it. It's never too early to start. Even if you're not looking for a job today, you never know what the future may bring. It's easier to request a donation from a contact with whom you've communicated for two years than from a person you've met once.

To tap into your network, you'll need to be clear about what you need and when you need it. Don't be shy about letting people know you are looking to grow your business, are open for new job opportunities, or are hoping for their charitable support for a fundraiser you're volunteering to organize. When you are networking properly and professionally, people will want to help you and see you succeed.

Give advance notice ahead of when you need their help. For example, if you've joined a fundraising committee, when you are engaged in conversation with contacts, let them know what you're doing. A simple "I'm volunteering for XYZ charity. Looks like we've got some great events coming this fall. I will definitely keep you posted as details are available" will subtly give them notice to expect your call.

This approach will help you get past a "gatekeeper" when you do call, because technically you can say that he's expecting to hear from you. If you're developing strong enough relationships, you should not have to worry about being screened by assistants because the person you're calling will want to take your call. It won't happen right away, but eventually this will be the reality.

Most of the time, people who like you, trust you, and believe you're competent will go out of their way to make a request from you a reality. If they can't help, they will at least be polite about the fact that they can't. They may even help you find someone who can or point you in the right direction.

When the first call you plan to make to a new contact is for a request, be sure you've established a mini-bond during your initial in-person introduction so your request won't seem way over the top. When you talk initially, set the expectation that you will call in hopes of getting them involved in a project. This up-front communication avoids any unnecessary surprises.

When you have a need, before looking to the Yellow Pages, consider who's in your network first. Who can help you? If you don't know, then who in your network would likely have a contact who could help you? Call the person to ask for a recommendation. It gives you a chance to connect and it gives your contact a chance to send a referral to someone in his or her network.

## Constantly ask yourself "Whom can I connect with whom?"

Constantly ask yourself "Whom can I connect with whom?"

Do people have problems that you can help solve? This is not an attempt at sainthood, but rather just a conscious effort to recognize challenges, identify needs, and find solutions for others around you.

When you make an effort to do this, first ask the people you are connecting if they would like to be connected. This way you'll avoid overstepping your boundaries by putting two people together when one or both are not interested in being connected. The safest option is to simply give a referral. "If you don't find anyone to solve your problem, it might be worthwhile to call so-and-so, who does this. Feel free to let him know you got his name from me."

There are formal and informal networking relationships. The bulk of your opportunities will be informal. These are the people in your network you may call from time to time, but there are no expectations attached to the association.

Formalized networking opportunities can be very advantageous to grow your business, provided each participant participates equally. Business clubs with the expectation to send each other referrals are great, but unfortunately far too often only one or two people will send referrals, whereas everyone else takes them.

You don't need to be a member of a business club to benefit from formalized referral activities. Partnering with like-minded, trusted professionals who offer complementary services can create a lifetime of positive business benefits, but again, only if the relationship is mutually beneficial.

This kind of a referral partnership should only be entered into if you share similar values for client service and have the capabilities to deliver an acceptable quality of service. Developing this kind of a coveted relationship is not to be taken lightly. As discussed earlier, offering a referral is an enormous gesture of trust.

When tapping into your network, be aware that each person in your network has a natural threshold for what he can offer to your relationship. Calling in a favor can have a domino effect if the person has to call one of his trusted contacts to help you.

Many professionals damage relationships by not respecting the goodwill expense it takes to make special requests happen. People are happy to help, but it's an important consideration to decide when, and to what degree, you can cash in on your influence and the resources of people in your network.

Those who have more substantial, meaningful relationships will have more clout when it comes to making requests and drawing on the goodwill of their relationships. That also means they'll likely be more guarded when it comes to making requests of people in their circles of influence.

A friend of mine went out of her way to arrange a private box at a premier sporting event for one of her associates. The fact that she could make it happen reflected her strong networking abilities and influence. At the last minute, her associate decided she didn't want the box anymore. In relationship terms, it was a disaster. My friend lost her influence and her shot to pull in a once-in-a-lifetime opportunity for someone who whimsically decided she didn't feel like going anymore.

To make matters worse, her associate didn't realize the magnitude of my friend's actions. She maxed out her goodwill threshold with a contact to cash in a major favor. It will be a long time before she can ask for another favor from him of that magnitude.

## When you make a request, be sure it is realistic in terms of what the person can give and reflects the depth of your relationship.

To continually return to the same person to ask for favors can deplete your relationship quickly. When you make a call for a major request, be sure it's worth it. When you're going to go for it, go for the gold. Just recognize what each person's "gold" threshold is in relation to your connection.

This concept is best explained when I reflect on my days as a professional fundraiser. My experience was that a relationship could get you in the door to make any request. It was up to you to seal the deal. Your success depended on how well you could judge what the appropriate donation request amount should be.

Asking for a $5,000 donation when a person was capable of $50,000 meant you left the opportunity for another $45,000 on the table. At the opposite end of the spectrum, if you went into the meeting requesting $50,000 when the donor's capacity to give was only $5,000, you would walk away with nothing because you asked for too much and made your potential donor feel uncomfortable.

Likewise, if you asked for $1,000 this month, but actually needed $2,000, you couldn't return to make an additional request from the same person the next month. However, if your initial request was for $2,000 over two months, you would arrive at the desired outcome.

My experience was primarily in annual fundraising and corporate sponsorships, so my philosophy was that I could ask potential donors for a large contribution once per year, provided I maintained and contributed to our relationship in between.

Networking relationships work the same way. You only get one shot to call in a major favor. Until you replenish the goodwill in the relationship bucket by returning the good deed, giving appropriate recognition, or sending business referrals, it's tricky to go back and ask for more.

When you make a request, be sure it is realistic in terms of what the person can give and reflects the depth of your relationship. Follow through on the request and always be sure to show appropriate appreciation.

# 60

# Staying Visible

TO MAXIMIZE YOUR NETWORKING EFFORTS, you'll have to stay top of mind for your contacts. You may recall that one of the two key objectives for networking, as discussed in Chapter 5, is to ensure that when your contacts have a need, they will think to call or recommend you first.

Once networking momentum is developed, it's easy to get a false sense of security and drop off the scene. This is dangerous because it will give your competition the opportunity to swoop in and take your place.

To stay at the forefront of your contacts' minds, either you need to interact with them or somehow they need to think about you when you're not there. You can't be everywhere and talking with everyone so finding strategies to keep you fresh in their thoughts is imperative to leverage your networking efforts.

The interaction part of the equation is easy. It's just time-consuming. It means staying visible by attending appropriate events and engaging in one-on-one networking activities. Every time you connect with a person, you re-establish yourself as a part of each other's network.

**To stay at the forefront of your contacts' minds, either you need to interact with them or somehow they need to think about you when you're not there.**

Keeping people thinking about you requires more creativity. When you can't be present, you still want the buzz about you to be there. This buzz, much like your reputation, is incredibly powerful when it is positive. Negative buzz can be equally powerful, but is detrimental.

There are several ways to raise your profile. Online networking is a huge source for visibility and has really leveled the playing field. You can be as front and center as you want to be with some strategic online effort. We'll discuss that in the coming chapter, but in the meantime, don't forget all of the traditional opportunities you have that can complement the most obvious source of publicity: the Internet.

The networking focus board that we will establish in Chapter 63: Finding Your Focus will assist you in deciding where to target your efforts for networking and profile building, as well as how to align your activities with your long-term objectives. By figuring out who you want to know, it's easier to decide how to become visible. Are you looking to appeal to the masses or to a specific sector?

For example, if you sell men's clothing, becoming a columnist for a women's fashion magazine is not advantageous unless your marketing strategy is to appeal to women to buy your product for the men in their lives.

## At the bare minimum, every professional should take a leadership role in a volunteer capacity.

At the bare minimum, every professional should take a leadership role in a volunteer capacity. Whether it's for a business association, a recreational activity, or a charitable cause, adding something of significance to your résumé will help you establish yourself in the community and expand your network.

It's more effective to be actively involved in one or two activities than to spread yourself too thin by joining multiple associations. You'll be able to use your focus board to establish the best places for you to invest your time.

Hosting annual company events is a great way to stay visible and raise your profile, provided you have the budget to do so.

An additional possibility is sponsoring events and looking for logo- and name-placement opportunities at functions that attract your target market. Each time a person notices your logo, especially when it is attached to a worthwhile cause, it will add to your goodwill bank account.

An effective way to stay top of mind is to develop a mass e-mail campaign or newsletter for your clients and contacts. These can be valuable tools, provided you follow some simple guidelines, as best laid out by Michael Hughes, a fellow networking consultant and president of Networking for Results.

I met Michael through this stay-in-touch technique when I launched my company. A local lawyer had been receiving his weekly e-tip for years, so when I told him about my plans to start my company, he forwarded me a copy of Michael's e-tip. Michael bases his e-tip on three simple criteria:

- value-based
- short
- permission-based

If you choose to set up an e-tip, e-zine, e-newsletter, or do something in print, these are valuable rules to follow. Even with the domination of social media posts, these types of proactive efforts still work, especially if you grow a huge list of followers who are engaged and interested in what you have to share.

Those who have a talent for writing have the opportunity to create a blog to showcase their knowledge and personality. Done properly, a blog will share content that will prove your competency and provide value for your readers and at the same time let your personality and nonwork-related interests shine. Social media can also help raise your profile and keep you visible in your network.

# 61

# Online Networking

As a consultant who originally focused only on teaching in-person networking strategies when my company was launched in 2006, I can't help but be fascinated by my own shift in attitude when it comes to online networking. It's been such a treat to study the nuances of online networking and how it impacts our IRL (in real life) relationships. The marketplace has changed so significantly over the last several years. If you don't have a comprehensive online strategy to complement your in-person networking efforts, you have a recipe for failure.

The technologies available to us are transforming every day and impact how we do business, but the foundational principles of business and networking don't change. In the first edition of *Business Cards to Business Relationships*, released in 2008, my comments on social networking sites only garnered a couple of paragraphs in the General Business Etiquette chapter, which seems unimaginable today. At the time, I wasn't a huge fan of online networking (which also seems unimaginable) because I'd built my network the old-fashioned way, making real, in-person connections.

As online networking sites grew in popularity I was asked by clients where they fit in the overall business-development strategy. My role as a columnist and blogger for Sun Media meant that I couldn't just ignore it as another trend that didn't interest me. I had to give online networking a chance to prove itself one way or another. I realized that by not actively participating in it and trying to make it work, I didn't have the right to slam it. So, a couple of years ago, I committed to giving online networking my best shot. Thankfully I did, because I have seen significant results from my efforts.

Everything throughout this book can be applied to your online networking as well as in-person efforts. Consider the four pillars of profitable networking as they could apply to online business development.

- **Perspective:** Online resources are one tool in your business-development arsenal. It will take time to build an engaged network. It can't be all one-way communication. For you to earn business online, just as in person, people need to like you, trust you, and believe you're competent. Technology can open doors for you that could never have happened without it, but relationship dynamics are the same online and offline.
- **Personal Brand:** What do people see, feel, and hear when they interact with your brand? When you interact or post online, you are influencing those three key elements and it's permanently stuck on the Web. Build your brand and protect it. Our lives are open books thanks to the Internet. Don't count on privacy settings. If you wouldn't want your new boss, your biggest client, or the media to see a post, don't post it.
- **Procedures:** Learn the different platforms and the etiquettes that apply to each. Don't interrupt conversations, but engage in them professionally. Use your online listening skills to monitor the pulse of your marketplace. Google yourself regularly because any new contact who is considering you as their service provider will google you. Know what they're going to find.
- **Strategic Plan:** There are more than 500 professional networking sites at the time of this book's printing and the list is growing. Strategically decide where your target market is and go there to connect. Your business plan should come first, then you can choose the most appropriate online tool that will help you fulfill your business plan. Online networking sites are excellent tools that let you research who knows who and connect the dots to success.

The reality is, business is global and it is open 24-7, so we need to find ways to accommodate this new reality and still create solid, trusting relationships. While online networking plays a huge role in business today, it does not replace the need to create face-to-face relationships. "High-touch" is as important today as "high-tech." There is something to be said for connecting in person. The Internet is an excellent tool to connect and meet people, but in the end, the majority (not all) of the closest, most trusted contacts in my network—and likely in yours—are the people you eventually meet and do business with face-to-face.

Imagine the different dynamic of a relationship once you've met someone you've tweeted with for a year at a conference. Online interactions played a role in facilitating the introduction and developing the relationship so you had the foundation to become fast friends in person.

Somehow you need to move online interactions beyond just reading each other's updates. It requires more substantial communication if you're looking to crack people's referral network and start landing major deals. While there are exceptions, huge corporations don't usually sign five- or six-figure contracts without having more than Twitter conversations with the consultant. At some point, they ask for a phone meeting or for you to fly out to meet the team.

Technology can help by changing the meaning of "face-to-face" interactions. It could equate to a webcam call over Skype, Google+, or another virtual meeting platform. Perhaps it is defined as an old-fashioned e-mail conversation or phone call.

For a professional service provider such as a lawyer, accountant, or investment advisor, online networking can help boost your brand, provide you links to prospects, and create credibility. When you use it for these purposes, you'll prosper. Embrace the fact that people will likely need to meet you in person before they have the comfort level to sign their life savings over to your control; whereas people who sell commodities such as T-shirts online don't require the same level of trust and therefore require less investment into the relationship before a buying decision is made.

Networking sites are an excellent place to connect and reconnect with contacts regardless of the depth of relationship you share. You can use the tools to stay on each other's radar screens and to facilitate a greater understanding of each other's service offerings and personalities.

Being linked electronically doesn't necessarily mean you'll do business with a person. How do you know if you like them, trust them, or believe they are competent? It's so easy to accept a "friend" request or invitation to "link" that there is very little consideration given to whether or not you'd actually recommend that person and consider him or her a valuable part of your official professional network. Being connected online doesn't equate to a long-term, mutually beneficial, and trusting business relationship.

Anyone can be anything online. Yes, people can pretend to be anything in person too, but at least when you have an in-person encounter you have a reference point from which to form an opinion. You have the natural warning signs, body language, and gut feelings that are generated through your interaction. That's not the case online. One saving grace is that because of the growing amount of information online, it's easy to do extra due diligence and get a pretty solid BS check before taking someone at face value.

Online networking offers huge volumes of contacts that never would have been possible for most people if they were just networking in person. With this comes greater responsibility and more risk, making it especially important that you manage your personal and company brands online.

## Don't confuse online followers with a profitable network.

While I think it's powerful to have lots of people in your online networks, don't confuse online followers with a profitable network. An online following and the kind of powerful network we're talking about in this book are two different things and serve two different purposes. You could have 10,000 names on a list, but that doesn't make it a profitable network. The real test is if you can pick up the phone and call in a favor from people on that list. If you call, will they answer?

Having a huge list of followers who consume your content is great, but that is not the same as creating a fulfilling network of quality contacts who develop into mutually beneficial business relationships. The celebrity model means they all know you, but you have no idea who they are except for an e-mail address—if that. While the celebrity model is profitable, unfortunately it's not attainable by everyone, whereas developing a solid profitable network of contacts built on mutual respect and connection is attainable for those who are willing to invest the time and effort required.

There are two philosophies to accepting friend requests and links online. Some choose to only accept people who they consider a trusted and treasured part of their professional network—others will accept almost anyone. Both are respected options and depending on your circumstances and desired outcome for online networking, you can choose the approach that works best for you.

The first philosophy basically means that if you wouldn't publicly endorse or recommend someone then you won't accept their friend request online. That means you'll have a smaller reach online, which means fewer people will learn about who you are, what you do, and what you have to offer. This approach assumes you are not using online to grow your network, but rather to nurture it. People seem to be moving away from this exclusive model, recognizing the power of reaching a larger audience.

My choice is the opposite. I'll accept almost everyone. That's in line with my overall business-development strategy. My work with a national news outlet pretty much means I lose my ability to control who reads my content, so in my opinion, the more the merrier. The more people who are exposed to my status updates, columns, and blog posts, the more likely it is someone who is planning a conference will think of me first when they want a speaker on personal branding or profitable networking. If I wanted to live a private life and keep my professional contacts close to my chest, then I wouldn't use online networking sites at all.

When you use the catch-all approach to online networking, as mentioned above, then it's important to make the distinction between online contacts and your treasured network. While there may be people I like and trust online, the people I would consider part of my trusted business network, 99 percent of the time, can also be listed in my personal and private database offline.

# 62

## Accessing the Traditional Media

WORKING IN THE MEDIA MAKES IT EASY TO stay visible. When I first started building my profile in the community, I didn't have this luxury. As I grew my contacts, I earned some media coverage for the organizations for which I worked and volunteered. Even before my official media roles, people could intermittently catch me on radio, on television, or in the newspaper. Then, once I became a regular columnist, the visibility grew. This profile proved to be an asset for other projects I had on the go.

A full-blown media career is not necessary for you to reap the benefits from the power of the press. Submitting interesting, relevant, and well-written columns to trade publications, local media, or industry associations for their newsletters can garner you quality profile in the community and with your target market.

News sources often have a list of experts they call for quotes when breaking news occurs. Develop relationships with your local media and make yourself easily accessible so they will think to call you. Obviously you must have substance, not just style, to keep these options alive and credible.

When media sources do call you, please be gracious and respond quickly. Many are so focused on getting out today's story that their turnaround time is pretty much immediate. I remember when I wrote my column four days a week. I'd call people and some would ask if they could have all the questions in advance and then connect with me next week after they'd had a chance to prepare. Next week? I'll be four stories past this by then. People who couldn't respond or tried to push their agenda didn't get asked again to comment.

Much like when networking, getting traction with traditional media outlets requires educating and connecting with your target market. In order to be considered, they need to know who you are, what you do, and what you have to offer. Plus, they need to sense that you're likeable. "Likeability" is less important than in the regular networking world, but if they *dislike* you, you definitely won't get called as a source. Media professionals need to trust you because they will shape their story based on the information you provide. If it isn't up to snuff, their credibility is called into question. They also have to believe you're competent otherwise they won't ask you to comment on a topic or give you the coverage.

When it comes to media, timing is everything. On a slow news day you may be able to get picked up just because they are looking for something different to cover. Just like on a heavy news day, your feel-good, nonurgent story can easily get bumped.

## When you speak to media sources: relax. Be confident by knowing your content and then try to be as natural as possible.

When you speak to media sources: relax. Be confident by knowing your content and then try to be as natural as possible. I have some horror stories of being on radio with my voice cracking and my mind going totally blank. Anyone who's listened to the radio can imagine how uncomfortable dead air is—imagine being the reason there is silence. So embarrassing. Despite having several of those occasions, I survived and bounced back to eventually learn how to speak on radio and television with ease. Just focus on having a conversation with the person doing the interview and forget about everyone listening. Try to avoid filler words such as "um" and "ah."

Make it easy for listeners to know who you are and what you're talking about. Avoid vague words. For example, instead of saying "At my company . . ." say "At ElevateBiz.com we . . ."

Whenever you send something to the media that you don't want edited, edit it yourself to the most basic, shortest format possible so they can't edit it any further. That way you can control the message and get the most important information through to the end story.

When you're interviewed, know the key messages you want to share and stick to communicating them succinctly. If you ramble on after saying your key points and share unimportant information, you'll give the editor too much information, forcing him or her to make cuts. He may not recognize the most important information that you want to share so he'll edit it down to a point that he sees as the best 10-second snippet. The editor is focused on ratings; you're focused on your message. If you want to get called back for more interviews, do your best to align your message with the station's desire to deliver interesting, relevant, and thought-provoking content to their listeners.

## When you're interviewed, know the key messages you want to share and stick to communicating them succinctly.

The whole point of getting media coverage is to give you credibility in your marketplace. It rarely sells your services, at least not until you've had several hits, but like any form of marketing and business-development strategy, networking will make it more powerful. Going to an event and having someone mention they heard you on the radio the other morning is a huge credibility booster.

Not getting the interview traction you'd like? Volunteer to be a guest host for your local radio and television stations. You can go one step further and purchase air time to host your own radio show, community television, or place an advertorial in the newspaper. Heck, you can even start blog-talk radio on one of the numerous Internet platforms available.

Going the route of having your own show is a huge amount of work. People rarely realize what it takes behind the scenes to produce a half-hour of quality content. In addition to creating and delivering the content, the bulk of the effort is getting people in your target market to see or hear your show. This is actually even more time-consuming than creating the show. Depending on your target market, your industry, and your personality, it can be time well invested. There's one financial advisor who does a weekly show explaining the markets. After a year he started to get recognized as a financial expert in public. After 18 months it became a profitable venture, as he's secured countless clients from his media activities.

Earned media is arguably the most powerful way to build profile and add credibility to your reputation, and ultimately, lead to a profitable network. So, if you can't become the show's host or no one will pick up your articles, don't beat yourself up too much. Case in point: I remember talking with a group of people at an event. They were all so excited that their associate had been featured in a two-page spread in the business section of the city's newspaper and asked if I had seen it. I didn't have the heart to tell them: I actually wrote the article. It just goes to prove, being the one sharing the story is not as important or as powerful as being the person who *is* the story.

If media doesn't appeal to you or won't help you achieve your objectives, there are plenty of other opportunities to create profile. It's not for everyone. Just find what aligns with your personality, will reach your target market, and makes sense for your overall business-development plan. If media is one of those elements, then great. Go for it!

# 63

## Finding Your Focus

WHEN I WROTE MY FIRST NEWSPAPER COLUMN, "People You Know," I had a rule: attend no more than seven events in one day. You may be thinking, "Yeah right, no more than seven events in one year." My recommendation is to meet somewhere at a comfortable place in the middle.

The point is that there is always something happening. There is always somewhere you could be and always another cause to support. To manage the possibilities, make filling your calendar a proactive activity, not a reactive one. Instead of responding to invitations solely based on your availability and whether or not you feel like attending, add strategy to your networking efforts to avoid the "mud-on-the-wall" approach mentioned earlier.

**To manage the possibilities, make filling your calendar a proactive activity, not a reactive one.**

There are six steps that will combine to create and maintain your personal focus board. This will make it easy for you to choose the right events to attend and to focus your networking efforts.

1. Define your desired outcome.
2. Clarify your target market.
3. Identify your interests and dislikes.
4. Commit your resources.
5. Create your focus board.
6. Check your activities.

## STEP 1: DEFINE YOUR DESIRED OUTCOME

From a business perspective, what are you hoping to achieve by building your professional network? Several networking benefits are listed below. Rate each benefit from 1 to 12 in order of importance to you.

- Raise company profile
- Raise personal profile
- Increase sales
- Increase referrals
- Gain access to specific target markets
- Find investors
- Achieve personal fulfillment
- Develop professionally
- Recruit new employees
- Help shape your industry
- Plan for company succession (transferring current business relationships to another person who will take over your company)
- Other

## STEP 2: CLARIFY YOUR TARGET MARKET

Whom do you need to meet? The best way to determine your target market is to write down your top five clients or connectors. Consider who they are, what makes them tick, and what specific qualities put them at the top of your list. Are there certain personality traits that draw you to these people? What do they do for work? What do they do for play? How do they spend their time? What causes do they support?

Who are the decision makers when it comes to buying your product or service? Who has the power to hire you or influence those who can? Those are the people you want to connect with on a regular basis. Going into a room full of people who have a problem to which you can provide the solution is where you'll find the gold mine of a profitable network.

The more you know about the characteristics of the person who can buy from you, the easier it will be to identify where you should go and with whom you should spend your time. It will also help you identify people who can move into your connector and target-market categories.

List your top five clients, then list their characteristics or activities.

## STEP 3: IDENTIFY YOUR INTERESTS AND DISLIKES

Getting involved in activities that make you miserable will make it difficult for you to connect because you'll be unhappy at the event. No matter how hard you try to mask your true feelings, people around you will sense your mood and will, consciously or subconsciously, avoid you.

Conversely, focusing your efforts on activities that align with your interests and passions can inject enthusiasm into your networking efforts.

**Focusing your efforts on activities that align with your interests and passions can inject enthusiasm into your networking efforts.**

A client talked about all the golf tournaments she was going to enter that summer. I was confused because I thought she disliked golf. Turns out, she couldn't stand the sport, but thought she had to golf to build her network. I wondered why.

Another client loathed working on dinner committees. She had organized her fair share of fundraising dinners and was good at it, thus she was asked to assist routinely. Much to her chagrin, she always felt compelled to say yes. That changed once we generated her focus board and she learned how to say no.

Make these clear distinctions so you won't get caught doing what you dislike. It doesn't mean you only get to do activities you love, but for the most part you can avoid the angst of participating in those that don't fit with your personality.

The list below can help you do this. Decide if you like, dislike, or are neutral about each type of networking activity. Then, you can build your entire networking strategy to avoid experiences you dislike while filling your calendar with activities that you enjoy or, at the very least, won't upset you.

- conventions
- lunches
- small dinner parties
- large dinner parties
- politics
- board of directorships
- formal dinner events

- committee work
- galas
- event organization
- charity events
- professional development
- award ceremonies
- dining clubs

- individual sports activities
- team sports involvement
- attending sporting events
- associations
- concerts
- service clubs
- theater
- book clubs
- speakers' forums

- cocktail parties and mixers
- coaching
- family outings
- golf tournaments
- golf games
- exercising
- business groups
- charity walks and runs
- issues-based causes

## STEP 4: COMMIT YOUR RESOURCES

To build your network you will have to participate in activities that connect you with people. This requires time and money. How much time and money you need to spend will depend on your goals, objectives, resources, and timeline. It will also depend on your personal and work commitments plus your bank account.

**To build your network you will have to participate in activities that connect you with people.**

To spend time with people who have money to invest or donate, you will have to go where people with money go—which will likely require more funding. To meet small start-up business owners who have less disposable income will require fewer financial resources.

Set an initial annual budget and review it after a few months. You may need to redirect resources from your advertising or direct-marketing budget to accommodate your new networking objectives.

How much time are you willing to invest to build your ultimate network? No doubt you are busy, but if your goal is to build a profitable network, you will have to set aside time to network.

A reasonable and effective pace is to commit to one or two business events and three one-on-one networking activities each week. There are times in the year when everything seems to happen all at once. Yet, there are other months when it feels like you're living in a ghost town. Make this cycle work in your favor. Slower times of the year are perfect times to connect one-on-one. You can have fewer one-on-one encounters when the event circuit is particularly heavy, as you will no doubt see contacts at events.

As you commit resources, determine if there are certain times that you simply can't or won't focus on business-network development. For example, Tuesday nights you play hockey and Sundays are family days. Write these boundaries on your focus board.

## STEP 5: CREATE YOUR FOCUS BOARD

Now we need to pull the above elements together to create your networking focus board. The idea is to have all of your networking activities align with your primary objective, your target market, your interests, and your resources of time and money. When an invitation crosses your desk and meets all of these criteria, then you know the activity is a good investment of your time. You can also use the focus board as a tool to be creative when filling your calendar.

You can download a focus board for free at www.BC2BR.com. Fill in the blanks on your focus board using the information from steps 1 to 4.

## STEP 6: CHECK YOUR ACTIVITIES

From now on, when an invitation crosses your desk, simply refer to your focus board and ask yourself: Would attending this function get me any closer to my goals and aspirations? Would my attendance there put me in front of my target market or people who are connected to them? Is this event one I would enjoy? Does this event match my time and money resources?

Going through this checklist each time you consider participating in a networking activity will help you focus your time, manage your finances, and make good decisions.

Enjoyable activities that do not fit your focus board should be considered social activities, not business networking activities. Yes, there are always hidden opportunities at the ball park because you don't know who'll be attending, but we want to purposefully put you into winning situations.

An event that doesn't meet at least three of the criteria on your focus board shouldn't be considered as a proactive, business networking opportunity. To begin your strategic approach, write down all of your current business-networking activities. Put each one through the focus board test. Which ones fit? Which ones don't fit?

Staying in your comfort zone and keeping busy with activities that don't fit your focus board is not a good time investment from a business perspective. Building a social network and a business network are two different priorities.

## If your priority is to increase sales, finding activities that attract a pool of potential clients makes good business sense.

If your priority is to increase sales, finding activities that attract a pool of potential clients makes good business sense. Spending all of your time at industry association meetings to build relationships with your competition doesn't.

If professional development is a top priority, then industry-related meetings that offer training and industry insight are definitely worthwhile.

An investment advisor, who spent the bulk of her networking time with one organization, wondered why she wasn't seeing a business return after years of building relationships within the group. When asked about her target market, it was clear that she wanted to attract individuals who met a certain investment threshold. We discovered that none of the members of the organization she belonged to had that kind of money available to invest. That was the reason for her lack of networking success.

The fundraiser who spends all her time meeting with other fundraisers and thinks she is busy networking is kidding herself. She may be having fun, but it's unlikely she'll find big donors in the mix.

You can't expect to turn contacts into business relationships if you're constantly surrounding yourself with people who don't qualify as potential buyers of your product or service.

# 64

# Filling Your Calendar

Now that you have a focus board, you can be proactive when developing your business networking plan. Research available opportunities for networking so you know where you want and need to be. Look at your city's networking circuit. You can google ideas, use an event-collection website such as www.meetup.com, or ask others in your target market for insight into the local networking scene. What's happening? What are the big events of the year? Where do the movers and shakers and your target market spend their time?

It may take you a year to get into the loop. You can't expect to be included on an invitation list for events you've never attended or expressed an interest in attending. As you hear about events that you missed, keep a log and plan to attend next time they occur.

The easiest way to find the best places to go is to ask members of your network the two vital questions we covered earlier.

1. Where should I go?
2. Whom should I meet?

Ask people you meet in one-on-one settings these questions and they will give you more than enough options to fill your calendar. Keep in mind, these contacts don't have access to your focus board, so don't feel you have to go everywhere that is suggested. Remember, check your focus board before you commit to any events or activities.

**Ask people: Where should I
go? Whom should I meet?**

Make a list of the top 20 business events in your city each year and build your calendar around those activities. Decide which are the ones that you must attend, should attend, or won't attend.

Next, look for obvious networking opportunities. Read the business section of the newspaper. Read trade journals and look for events and conferences that will attract your target market. Is there an industry association that serves your target market where you can get involved? Are there charities that interest you and meet your focus-board criteria? Are there causes that you're passionate about that would attract like-minded people?

Don't stop finding networking opportunities until your calendar reflects your goal of one to two formalized business activities and three one-on-one meetings per week. Refer to your list of connectors. With whom do you want to meet first? Are there people you should reconnect with right away? Once you've blocked off time for networking meetings, call your contacts and fill your calendar.

A great way to fill your calendar is to look to your interests and find a way to align those with your target market. Sometimes it takes some imagination, but understand that networking doesn't always have to be someone else's initiative. You can take your own.

## Fill your calendar by looking at your interests and find a way to align those with your target market.

For example, a friend loved to host dinner parties and loved to meet new people. So, every Wednesday night she opened her home for a dinner party. The only rule was you had to let her know the day before if you were coming and you were asked to bring a bottle of wine. She took care of the rest. Imagine, every week there was a different group of people around her dining room table.

Do you love skiing? Why not start a weekly ski group that travels to a nearby resort every week or once a month? In my city there is a group of professionals who go skiing together once a week for the entire season and over the years have become great friends. At some point, someone had to start the group activity.

One of my favorite initiatives is by the women in a firm. They started a quarterly women's roundtable discussion group. They invite 100 women to attend one of three meals where there is a facilitated discussion on an interesting topic concerning business and today's workplace. It's an incredibly enjoyable experience with a different group dynamic each time. Plus, it shows the firm's credibility by leading conversations around relevant topics.

Just have some fun with it. Determine what you love to do and see how you could create something to pull your target market together. Whatever you do, be sure you're not duplicating something else that's already happening well in your area. It may be just as easy to join an established young professionals' wine-tasting club than to start your own.

Yes, there will be days when you won't feel like networking or when you're too busy to go out for lunch, but I suspect there are days when you don't feel like going to work and yet you still do. You have to go to work; it's how you earn your living.

Now that you're learning how to network properly and professionally, networking will directly contribute to the ease in which you can achieve success. Before long, connecting with others will become second nature and will be a high priority in your calendar.

# 65

# Analyzing the Options

NETWORKING OPPORTUNITIES ARE everywhere. They are on the subway, in your office elevator, or on the street. Just leaving your house each day makes you eligible for great chance encounters. Everyone has at least one random introduction success story. Keep your head up when you're in public, be open to meeting new people, and be aware of potential opportunities.

Since this book is designed to help you develop a proactive networking approach for long-term profitable results, we will leave the chance encounters to chance and focus on the formalized options that can help you build your network.

The more involved you become, the more you will notice an increase in invitations and requests for support. Using your focus board will allow you to choose the best activities for you.

**The more involved you become, the more you will notice an increase in invitations and requests for support.**

As you develop your professional network, you will find what works for you and what activities you truly enjoy. Below are some perspectives on various networking opportunities to help you make decisions about how to best invest your time and money. As a rule of thumb, the later in the day you network, the more expensive it is and the larger the time investment. For example: breakfast is cheaper than lunch, lunch is cheaper than after-work drinks,

drinks are cheaper than dinner, and dinner is cheaper than entertaining clients at an evening event such as the theater or a hockey game.

A good mix of all of these options is ideal, with more time and money being invested with those whom you want to build the deepest relationships.

**Breakfast meetings** give you an early start to your day. They get your networking out of the way so you don't have to interrupt your workday. Breakfast is usually reasonably priced so if your budget is tight, this is a sensible option.

**Lunch meetings** are a great way to break up your day. Find your favorite lunching hot spots so you know what to expect in terms of food, service, and price. Lunch meetings are a solid opportunity for casual one-on-one discussions that deepen your professional connections. Also, you will likely run into other professionals while lunching. Official business discussions tend to happen after the main meal. It is difficult to eat and look at business papers at the same time.

Be prepared to pick up the check. It can get a little pricey unless you're meeting with people who have company expense accounts. Taking turns is very acceptable and more professional than splitting the bill unless your lunch is with a close friend or associate with whom you eat regularly. If a person insists on paying, it is appropriate to accept someone else's generosity. A thank-you note after the fact adds a nice touch.

**Coffee meetings** are quick, easy, informal, and inexpensive. Have coffee meetings in your office to maximize your time or find a comfortable coffee shop close to your workplace.

**Virtual coffee meetings** are great. They're a good old-fashioned phone call and so much easier to schedule when two busy people want to get caught up or when you're traveling a lot for business. Plan for a half-hour conversation and treat it the same way you would any coffee meeting. Balance the virtual coffee with some personal get-to-know-you chitchat and business talk. Same results, but with less time needed to get to and from the meeting.

**Charity functions** are a superb place to meet people while supporting a worthwhile cause. Complete your pre-event homework before you go so you have an idea of who will be there. Who is sponsoring the event? Who volunteers for the charity?

Watch your budget. Costs at these events can add up quickly, especially when charities encourage you to spend money at the function in addition to the ticket price. Senior-level management and executives are often in the room so it's a worthwhile investment to attend if they are your target market. Practice your mingling skills before you go so you can have short, strong conversations that will plant the seed for the follow-up outside the event. Senior executives do not want to be "sold" at an event. When you're there with them, treat yourself as an equal.

**Industry-related associations** provide many rewarding opportunities to shape the future of your industry. You can learn from your peers and network effectively. Associations give you a chance for professional development and opportunities to sink your teeth into projects, all of which can earn you a reputation as a go-to person. Through your involvement in the association, you can earn recognition as a leader in your industry. Just be sure your potential customers see that as well, not just your peers and competition.

**Committee work** is a very hands-on approach that will allow you to make a positive impact on a project and raise your profile. There are always more than enough opportunities around for good volunteers. Use these committee meetings to establish your reputation as someone who delivers. Strive to under-promise and over-deliver.

**Serving on boards** is an appealing way to shine in the community. Your involvement on a board would provide an excellent opportunity to do some rewarding work and add something impressive to your résumé. Before making the commitment (minimum two years, but likely six), ensure you understand all the expectations. What are the time and financial commitments? Are you responsible for raising funds? If so, would you be comfortable doing that?

**Special interest groups** attract like-minded people. People united for a cause, such as politics, religion, or the environment, are likely to form deep connections because they already have core beliefs in common. Joining the local environmental group, even though it may not specifically serve your target market, can lead to expanded circles of influence.

A friend, Dean, was hired by a law firm. His boss was particularly excited about Dean's extracurricular activities, as he saw huge potential for him to bring referrals to the firm. For years Dean had taken leadership roles in both the political realm and the gay community. Much to his own surprise as a young lawyer, all of the business he brought to the firm has been a direct result of the networks developed through his involvement with these two causes.

**Business networking groups and clubs** operate with the expectation that everyone is there to connect for business. Before joining such a group, attend a couple of meetings as a guest. Do you feel comfortable? What's the tone of the group? Is your competition a member or would you be the only representative from your industry? Do members do business together? Would you be likely to recommend the members to your contacts? If not, don't join. What are the expectations of membership? Are the fees, if applicable, appropriate for your budget?

Can't find the right networking club? Why not start your own? Some of the most productive networking groups originated thanks to like-minded people coming together with the specific intention to build relationships and send each other referrals. Each month the group meets and each member has to report on his interaction with other members.

Caution: business groups and associations can become comfort zones. It's easy to go back to meetings week after week before realizing you're in a networking rut. Staying with a group when you're not enjoying it, especially if it doesn't fit your focus board or isn't leading to business relationships, is not a wise investment for you. Don't be afraid to change your choice of activities every couple of years.

**Conventions and trade shows** by their very nature attract people with similar interests. They are a great place to learn about your competitors, resources, and innovations. Pre-event homework is imperative to make these events worthwhile, especially since they often require travel and a time commitment of up to several days. Make a list of whom you want to meet.

For annual events, call or e-mail contacts in advance to let them know you'll be there and that you look forward to seeing them. If there is specific business to discuss, let them know in advance that you would like to meet for a coffee sometime over the course of the trade show or event.

Visit the hospitality suites and mingle to meet and reconnect with contacts. Avoid spending the whole convention in your comfort zone talking with your work colleagues.

To really get your company noticed, consider sponsoring a portion of the convention, providing refreshments during the breaks, or hosting your own hospitality suite. As an individual, taking a leadership role on the organizing committee can get you noticed and make it easier for you to meet conference attendees.

**Private golf games** require significant time and financial investment (depending on where you play), but can be worthwhile provided you pick your partners well and you are able to keep your composure for extended periods of time. Golf games are great when you are looking to establish or deepen a professional relationship with a specific person.

A lot can be said about a person's character by how he or she lets a little white golf ball affect his or her day. If you have a tendency to kick the ball from the rough onto the fairway using a "foot wedge," throw your club, or refuse to count *all* your putts, then avoid taking business contacts on the golf course.

Remember, you want people to like you, trust you, and believe you are competent. Emotional golfers or those who routinely and conveniently forget to follow the hard and fast rules of golf lose credibility on the course, which, in turn, detracts from their perceived credibility in the boardroom.

Business talk is usually kept to a minimum, but the relationship built over a fun, relaxing golf game can lead to closed deals. If you do choose to golf, be sure to learn the rules of golf etiquette. Here are just a few:

- Count all your shots.
- Don't talk while someone is on the tee box, putting, or taking a shot.
- Don't use your cellphone on the course.
- Keep pace of play with your golf mates and the foursome in front of you.
- Wear the appropriate regulation golf attire.

**Golf tournaments** can create bonds, but primarily with the three others in your foursome. Shower quickly after the game and stick around for dinner so you can maximize time to connect with others at the tournament. Don't spend all the time before and after your round with your same foursome. You'll have plenty of time to connect with them during the game and at the dinner.

Unless it's a staff bonding day, sharing a cart with a colleague is not a wise investment of time or money. Try to share a cart with a potential client or new contact. Be prepared to lose an entire day out of the office to attend a tourney.

Golf tournaments rarely help your golf swing; the best ball format can make it frustrating for those who take the game too seriously.

The rules of the game still need to be respected, even though it's a fun day on the course. Keep alcohol consumption to a minimum.

# 66

## Networking Ruts

NETWORKERS INEVITABLY GET COMFORTABLE. They'll hang with the same people, go to the same places, and have the same conversations over and over and over again. A comfort zone is created and once that happens it's easy to get stuck and miss opportunities. It's as if the enthusiasm to grow their network ends and the professional settles into habits that don't include recognizing and embracing new opportunities and relationships.

While it's nice to nurture current relationships, growth helps a network thrive. Mixing and mingling with the new recruit at your service club and making him or her feel welcomed will go a long way to positively impacting another's life, and yours at the same time.

### When a comfort zone is created, it's easy to get stuck.

I've had the good fortune to attend and speak at many association meetings. The dynamics are pretty predictable:

- The "forever-member" leaders act like they run the place—and they do. Most likely quote from them is "Well, that's how we've always done it."
- The "new vibe" leaders are actively trying to bring new ways of doing things to the organization. They usually put in hours above and beyond expectations with hopes of seeing their vision come to fruition—eventually.
- The "even-longer-than-forever" members have given up on running the organization, but come to meetings faithfully to reconnect with a handful of colleagues.

- The "really-don't-want-to-be-here" members attend to put in their time because it's their job requirement. They expect zero benefit from membership and hit their target of zero benefit every year.
- The "eager-beaver" newbies are determined to make the group a positive and profitable experience, but often feel shut down. Eventually they lose their enthusiasm because they can't get in with the establishment.
- Then there is everyone else.

Can you see how, with these dynamics, people can miss opportunities to derive true value from the organizations they belong to for years? Each group is obvious to me because they all mingle with each other during the cocktail hour and then sit together for the formal part of the session. Once the cliques and stagnant routines are that obvious to an outsider, you know a group networking rut has been created.

Imagine if newbies were paired with an old-timer. What if, instead of the leadership sitting at the head table looking out over the group, they split up and each director sat at a different table to mix with the general membership? How about encouraging people to find new synergies within the group and for members to meet outside regular group meetings so they can get to know each other better? Have you ever considered a "hot seat" where a member could present a business growth challenge and the membership all contribute ideas? Why not have members introduce themselves by sharing something other than their name and company name? It could be a personal tidbit, their biggest challenge, or the type of leads that work best for them. Whatever, just something that takes the introduction time beyond a roll call and creates some depth of understanding as to who is part of the membership.

As a leader in your organization or in your office, or as the owner of your company, take responsibility for recognizing these networking ruts and doing something to change them.

Even when it comes to interacting and nurturing relationships with clients, it's easy to pick our favorites and spend all of our time focused on them instead of growing the next layer of relationships. When categorizing your contacts and developing your relationship-management action plans, take special note if you are repeating the same-old same-old all the time. Are you seeing one client 10 times a year, whereas you see others once or twice? It happens a lot with professionals. Recognizing the pattern is the first step to changing old habits. You have two choices: do more with other clients or limit your time with those who are monopolizing your time.

# Summary

## *The Fourth Pillar of Profitable Networking: Strategic Plan*

- Ask contacts the vital questions: Where should I go? Whom should I meet?
- Use an electronic filing system for tracking contacts.
- Develop a user-friendly system to categorize your contacts so you can identify proper pace for follow-up and next steps for relationship management.
- Find ways to remain visible to your network. Don't fall off the radar screen, thus giving your competition the chance to create mini-bonds with your contacts.
- Follow through with your commitments.
- Once relationships are built, make a concerted effort to maintain and nurture them.
- Check potential networking events against your focus board. Activities that don't fit your criteria are not considered priority areas for building your professional network.
- Be proactive and strategic about your networking efforts.
- Proactively fill your calendar with opportunities to connect with people.
- Analyze the options available and make good strategic decisions about where to invest your resources. Avoid networking ruts. Expand your comfort zone to keep your networking fresh.

# Epilogue

_____

## *Become the Ultimate Connector and Make Your Mark!*

THE GENTLEMAN WHO SPARKED my passion for networking (remember the lawyer who took me to my first committee meeting?) is considered by many to be the quintessential networker or, as I liked to call him, the ultimate connector.

He took great pleasure in helping others build their business networks. He had a habit of taking young professionals under his wing, showing them the way, and then freeing them to make life happen with the people they meet. I have wondered what my life would be like today if I hadn't met him on that pivotal Saturday morning when I was 25 years old.

When he was alive, I thanked him on various occasions for changing my life, but he was reluctant to accept my praise. He didn't feel that it was necessary to thank him because he believed that helping others was just the right thing for him to do. There are plenty of his "recruits" who attributed the start of their networks to him. In the truest sense of the word, he was a "connector."

The only thing he asked in return is that we go on to become successful contributing members of the community. In his early 80s he still represented his law firm in the community and I'm sure his networking efforts earned business for the firm, but being or becoming a client was never a stipulation of his generosity to others.

It's amazing how much we can impact someone's life by simply starting a conversation and connecting them to positive people. Aligning ourselves with those we like and trust and who feel the same way about us leads to powerful outcomes.

Knowing lots of people, as we established throughout the book, is not enough. At some point you need to get out of the networking events and deliver your product or service. Focus on providing solutions to your contact's problems and if you do that, you can't help but be profitable. Business at its most basic form is simply Problems + Solutions = Revenue. Genuinely connect with people, find the problems your product or service solves, and you will make a difference.

Imagine being that person for someone else—a true connector. Imagine changing another's day for the better or altering another's life thanks to an introduction you made. When you consider it a priority to bring people together, the possibilities are endless. These good deeds will inevitably boomerang to reward you when you least expect it.

Looking back on my life, there are several people who fall into this ultimate connector category. These are the people who genuinely want others to prosper and it's amazing to know these people. They go out of their way to make others feel comfortable and to help them find success. Their lives are spent looking beyond themselves and inevitably success and fulfillment follow them.

Your path to a profitable network begins with you becoming an ultimate connector. Start by noticing what people in your network need, even just the little things. Filling even those small needs can have a profound impact. Bring people together to work for a common goal and set people up for success. Your rewards will follow. Having a generous spirit with others and taking your eyes off your own personal needs may not have immediate results, but these actions will contribute to an unsurpassed quality of life.

You will earn a reputation as someone who networks well and you will be differentiated from those who don't. When you surround yourself with great people, great things happen—that's how the universe works. If you can do that, the profits will follow.

It is my belief that the most satisfying aspect of networking is becoming part of someone else's success story.

# Stay Connected with Allison Graham and ElevateBiz

DON'T LET YOUR PROFITABLE networking journey stop here. This is just the beginning.

Just scan this QR code or visit www.BC2BR.com/book for a mobile experience designed just for readers of *From Business Cards to Business Relationships: Personal Branding and Profitable Networking Made Easy,* Second Edition.

You'll find special videos to watch, worksheets to download, and recommended reading. There's a place to share your networking stories, give feedback, and receive the ElevateBiz EBlasts.

If you are interested in having Allison Graham speak for your company or at an upcoming conference: all the info is right there waiting for you!

**PLUS you could WIN online coaching with Allison Graham!**

# About the Author

Allison Graham is the force behind Elevate Seminars + Strategic Development Inc., a business strategy company that teaches professionals how to develop valuable business relationships from casual business card contacts. Her work as a keynote speaker, corporate trainer and business consultant has helped thousands of professionals catapult their business skills to raise their community profile, penetrate new circles of influence and open doors for revenue growth opportunities.

Mastering the art of networking was what took Allison from working in a mediocre job and feeling like a stranger in a new city, to where she is today with thousands of contacts and an impressive track record in business, media, politics and the charitable and non-profit sectors. Allison attributed her progress to learning how to network and made it her personal mission to help other professionals learn how to get connected regardless of their circumstances. Allison pens the column, "Getting Connected: The Art of Networking" for Sun Media, plus has contributed to several media sources on the topics of personal branding and profitable networking. Prior to writing her current business-focused column, Allison was the "People You Know" columnist for the *London Free Press* for four years. Writing four columns a week and interacting with thousands of people at hundreds of events each year gave her a unique vantage point of the city's business and philanthropic communities. This intense involvement was the inspiration for many stories in this book.

As an active member of the community, Allison has been involved with several worthwhile causes and charitable organizations. She is a professional member of the Canadian Association of Professional Speakers (CAPS) and the Global Speakers Federation (GSF). Elevate Seminars + Strategic Development Inc. is a proud member of the Better Business Bureau.

Allison was raised in Erie Beach, Ontario. In 1992 she attended Albert College where she graduated with honors. After this time in Belleville she moved to London, Ontario to attend Huron University College at Western University. She has made London her home ever since and loves to spend time with family, friends and her dog Winston C.

www.ElevateBiz.com
305-611 Wonderland Rd. N.
London, ON, Canada
N6H 5N7